Produced in cooperation with The Greater Springfield Chamber of Commerce.
Photo by Terry Farmer

Library of Congress Cataloging-in-Publication Data

Mann, Curtis, 1968-
Greater Springfield : where tradition meets tomorrow / by Curtis Mann and Edward J. Russo ; corporate profiles by Melinda Garvert ; featuring the photography of Terry Farmer ; produced in cooperation with the Greater Springfield Chamber of Commerce.— 1st ed.
    p. cm.
  Includes index.
  ISBN 1-58192-049-0
    1. Springfield Region (Ill.)—Economic conditions. 2. Industries—Illinois—Springfield Region. 3. Springfield Region (Ill.)—Pictorial works. 4. Springfield Region (Ill.)—History. I. Russo, Edward J. II. Garvert, Melinda, 1945- . III. Farmer, Terry, 1959- . IV. Greater Springfield Chamber of Commerce (Ill.) V. Title.
HC108.S798 M36 2002
977.3'56—dc21
                        2001005474

Photo by Terry Farmer

The Greater Springfield Chamber of Commerce and Community Communications, Inc.,
would like to express our gratitude to these companies for their leadership in the development of this book.

Photo by Terry Farmer

Greater Springfield
WHERE TRADITION MEETS TOMORROW

By **CURTIS MANN AND EDWARD J. RUSSO**
Corporate Profiles by **MELINDA GARVERT**
Featuring the photography of **TERRY FARMER**

Community Communications, Inc.
Publisher **RONALD P. BEERS**

Staff for *Greater Springfield:*
Where Tradition Meets Tomorrow

Acquisitions	**HENRY S. BEERS**
Publisher's Sales Associate	**MEL MERK AND KAREN PETERSON**
Editor in Chief	**WENDI LEWIS**
Managing Editor	**MARY CATHERINE RICHARDSON**
Editorial Assistants	**DEBRA C. CARROLL AND KREWE MAYNARD**
Design Director	**SCOTT PHILLIPS**
Designer	**EDDIE LAVOIE**
Photo Editors	**EDDIE LAVOIE AND MARY CATHERINE RICHARDSON**
Pre-Press and Separations	**DCR GRAPHICS**
National Sales Manager	**KEELY SMITH**
Sales Assistants	**BRANDON MADDOX AND ANNETTE LOZIER**
Accounting Services	**STEPHANIE PEREZ**

CCI

Community Communications, Inc.
Montgomery, Alabama

DAVID M. WILLIAMSON Chief Executive Officer
RONALD P. BEERS President
W. DAVID BROWN Chief Operating Officer

© 2001 Community Communications
All Rights Reserved
Published 2001
Printed in USA
First Edition
ISBN: 1-58192-049-0
Library of Congress Catalog Number: 2001005474

Terry Farmer photos © 2001
www.terryfarmer.com

Every effort has been made to ensure the accuracy of the information herein. However, the authors and Community Communications are not responsible for any errors or omissions that might have occurred.

Front and back cover images by Terry Farmer

Photo by Terry Farmer

table of contents

Foreword, 10
Preface, 12
Part One, 14

EDUCATIONAL EXCELLENCE 54
From the first subscription schools in the 1820s, Springfield has made a solid commitment to educating its people whether it is a child starting kindergarten or an adult seeking a professional degree. The blend of schools with public and private colleges and universities offers the people of Springfield and the surrounding area many choices for an education.

LAND OF LINCOLN 16
Springfield embraces the legacy of Abraham Lincoln and has preserved his memory for the world to see. His home, tomb, and other sites remind the people of the mark Lincoln left on a town that would preserve his contributions to America.

HEALTH CARE LEADER 64
Springfield provides its residents with excellent availability of state-of-the-art medical care, from family physicians to specialized treatment for serious illnesses. Today health care services form a major sector of the city's economy, second only to government in size.

HISTORY 24
From business to transportation, medicine to religion, Springfield has been shaped by her many generations of people. Since its founding in 1821, commerce and government have played a key role in the development of the city.

THINGS TO SEE AND DO 74
Taking a jog in Washington Park, riding the skydiver on the Midway at the Illinois State Fair, attending a concert at the Sangamon Auditorium—these are all things residents and guests are drawn to in Springfield. Whether a guest to the city or a long-time resident, Springfield promises to entertain!

A CAPITAL ATTRACTION 32
Springfield serves as the center of government for the state of Illinois. Laws are created, citizens serve as state employees, and decisions that affect every person in Illinois are made right here in the capital city.

CENTRAL SUCCESS 42
The agricultural wealth developed many years ago has been a firm foundation for Springfield to develop its diverse economy. The entrepreneurial spirit of its founders has created a sense of economic development over the last generation that continues to allow Springfield to thrive with success.

Springfield 9

A SPECIAL SPIRIT 86

An act of kindness by a neighbor or church member or an anonymous donation to a charity all help to make Springfield the livable place it is. From helping an adult learn to read for the first time to building a Habitat for Humanity house, Springfield is a place rich in community spirit.

HIGH TECHNOLOGY, NETWORKS & UTILITIES 100

Insight Communications, 102-103
Cingular Wireless, 104-105
CIBER, 106
Springfield Mass Transit District, 107
Levi, Ray & Shoup, Inc., 108
Yevich, Lawson and Associates, Inc., 109
CILCO, 110

MANUFACTURING & DISTRIBUTION 112

Brandt Consolidated, Inc., 114-115
Nudo Products, Inc., 116-117
Solomon Colors, 118
Mel-O-Cream Donuts International, 119
Phoenix International, 120

11

BUSINESS, FINANCE & THE PROFESSIONS 122

Express Personnel Services, 124-125
The Greater Springfield Chamber of Commerce, 126-127
Kerber, Eck & Braeckel LLP, 128-129
Sorling, Northrup, Hanna, Cullen and Cochran, Ltd., 130-131
Hanson Professional Services Inc., 132-133
Staab Funeral Home, 134
Resource One, 135
HIP Advertising, 136
Illinois National Bank, 137
Kirlin-Egan & Butler Funeral Home and Cremation Tribute Center, 138
Standard Mutual Insurance Company, 139
The Horace Mann Companies, 140
Systemax Corporation, 141

HEALTH CARE & EDUCATION 142

University of Illinois at Springfield, 144-145
Doctors Hospital, 146
Lincoln Land Community College, 147
Robert Morris College, 148

13

REAL ESTATE, DEVELOPMENT & CONSTRUCTION 150

Siciliano, Inc., 152-155
FWAI Architects Inc., 156-157
Orchard Park Apartments, 158-159
R.D. Lawrence Construction Company, LTD., 160
Perry Broughton Trucking & Excavating, Inc., 161
Vancil Contracting Inc., 162
P.H. Broughton & Sons, Inc., 163

THE MARKETPLACE, HOSPITALITY & TOURISM 164

Renaissance Hotel, 166-167
Springfield Convention and Visitors Bureau, 168
White Oaks Mall, 169

Part Two, 98
Enterprise Index, 170
Bibliography, 172
Index, 173

Photos by Terry Farmer

Foreword

Forward thinking, leadership, unprecedented collaboration between the public and private sectors, and an engaged populace have combined to make this a defining moment in the long, rich history of Greater Springfield.

Not since the City of Springfield was named the Capitol of Illinois, nor since its favorite son, Abraham Lincoln, was elected President, has there been a time when the community was in the limelight and poised for positive change as it is at the beginning of this new millennium.

Offering its residents a low cost of living, excellent public services, a growing and diverse community, a broad range of cultural and recreational opportunities, a major medical center, and outstanding educational institutions, Greater Springfield defines what "quality of place" is really all about.

Greater Springfield: Where Tradition Meets Tomorrow traces the evolution of this community and its major businesses and institutions and describes just why its future holds so much promise. The words and images which follow describe its history, economy, attractions, and its most important asset: its people.

The Greater Springfield Chamber of Commerce is pleased to partner with Community Communications, Inc. in the production of this quality publication. We trust that the reader, whether a resident, visitor, or other friend, will discover those things which make Springfield a truly special and unique place to invest, live, work, and play.

Michael Boer
President/CEO
The Greater Springfield Chamber of Commerce

Photo by Terry Farmer

Preface

In our work as local historians at Lincoln Library we have the great fortune to merge our passion for history with our daily work. The Sangamon Valley Collection is Springfield's repository for local information, both current and historic. Our job is to collect, organize, and disseminate this information about our community. We continually discover new aspects of Springfield's rich history while helping customers, whether they are looking for ancestors, house histories, lost classmates, or Route 66 legends and lore. Because Springfield is a city nostalgic about its past it seemed natural for us to write the half-dozen photographic histories about our town. When the chance came to profile present-day Springfield we were excited about the prospect. It is challenging to look at the place we live and work. When one is close to a subject it is difficult to see it with an unbiased eye. By consciously trying to distance ourselves a bit, we were fascinated to discover the diversity of our economy, the range of business, and the wealth of cultural, athletic, and entertainment opportunities.

While we bring a shared historical perspective to our descriptions of contemporary Springfield, we also bring separate and personal points of view. These different perspectives and experiences influenced (we think positively) the way in which we wrote. The fact that we are almost a generation apart, one a native, the other a recent resident, gives the story both "insider" and "newcomer" frames of reference.

The task of producing a book of this type is made infinitely easier through the network of people coordinating its creation. The Greater Springfield Chamber of Commerce, its President/CEO Mike Boer, its board, and membership, were invaluable partners. Talented Springfield photographer Terry Farmer created beautiful and evocative images of the city. Local businesses went the extra distance to tell their stories in the profiles section.

For us, telling the story of *Greater Springfield: Where Tradition Meets Tomorrow* has truly been, our pleasure.

Edward J. Russo
Curtis Mann

Photo by Terry Farmer

Part One

Photo by Terry Farmer

chapter | one

1

LAND OF LINCOLN

The image of Lincoln pervades the city in history and the present day. Lincoln in bronze by sculptor Andrew O'Connor holds silent watch over visitors and residents in front of the Capitol. Photo by Terry Farmer

The interior of Lincoln's tomb reflects a complete restyling from 1931 by state architect C. Herrick Hammond in which a miscellany of photos and "memorabilia," that once cluttered the structure were swept away—replaced by this simple, chaste setting. Carloads of marble, bronze, gold plating, and brushed metalwork ceilings outfitted the new spaces in a dignified version of moderne and art deco-inspired design. Photo by Terry Farmer

Springfield lives and breathes Abraham Lincoln. His name is proliferated in numerous buildings and businesses throughout the city. And Lincoln is synonymous with tourism. The city has embraced his legacy and preserved his memory for the world to see. The Lincoln home, tomb, law office, and other sites have been restored and maintained to help people catch a glimpse of his life in Springfield. Markers abound in the downtown noting connection to this place or that—his family pew at First Presbyterian Church, the old courthouse where he practiced law, and significantly, the Old State Capitol where he delivered his famous "House Divided Speech." Springfield's efforts to present Lincoln to the world continue with an ambitious $150 million presidential library and museum scheduled for completion in 2003.

The public's fascination with Abraham Lincoln began soon after his nomination to the presidency in 1860 when reporters, colleagues, and well-wishers flocked to the modest house at the northeast corner of 8th and Jackson streets to learn how the new presidential candidate lived. Even after his departure for Washington D.C., visitors continued their pilgrimages—from traveling businessmen to soldiers from nearby Camp Butler, an almost constant parade streamed past the home. After Lincoln's assassination his memory grew to legendary proportions overshadowing every other resident before or since. Visitors continued streaming to the house in greater numbers each year. The home remained in the Lincoln family until Robert Todd Lincoln donated it to the State of Illinois in 1887. The now world-famous dwelling and surrounding blocks became a national park in 1974 when President Richard Nixon traveled to Springfield for a ceremony marking its transfer to the federal government and making it the only national park in Illinois. The house was completely renovated in 1988 with the surrounding four-block area being carefully restored to recreate, as much as possible, its appearance in Lincoln's day.

After President Lincoln's assassination, his grieving widow, Mary, recalling how her husband loved the peace and beauty of Springfield's Oak Ridge Cemetery, agreed to have him buried there. A monument was constructed where Lincoln, his wife, and three of his children were eventually buried. The twice-reconstructed tomb has become a national shrine, visited by dignitaries and hundreds of thousands of others, making it the second most visited site in Springfield. Today, people from all around the world come to pay their respects and rub the shiny nose of the tomb's Lincoln bust for good luck.

Centered on the city's historic downtown square, the Old State Capitol, famous as the site for Lincoln's "House Divided" Speech, was completely disassembled and rebuilt in the late 1960s by the state of Illinois.

Abraham Lincoln impersonators in the capital city come in all ages, shapes, and sizes including this young visitor to the Illinois State Fair, complete with stovepipe hat and flags flying. Photo by Terry Farmer

The kitchen of Abraham Lincoln's home gives a glimpse into life behind the parlor in 19th century America. The wood-burning stove was a vast improvement over open fireplace cookery. Mary Lincoln was an exacting housekeeper as many a "hired girl" soon discovered. The Lincoln dining room (opposite, below) shows the more formal aspect of mid-Victorian life with its china, damask cloth, and flowered wallpaper. Photos by Terry Farmer

Abraham Lincoln's home is set in a restored neighborhood of 19th century houses and is visited by more than 400,000 people every year. The home has been a magnet for tourists ever since Lincoln was elected president. His son, Robert Todd Lincoln, donated the house to the State of Illinois, which cared for it until 1972 when it was deeded over to the United States of America. Today, under the care of National Park Service staff, the house has been meticulously restored so that it would be familiar to the Lincoln family. Photo by Terry Farmer

Today it appears as it did when Lincoln was a legislator there. Costumed interpreters take visitors through the various offices and chambers explaining how state government was managed 160 years ago. A Nineteenth Century Children's Fair is a popular, family-oriented event held during the Fourth of July on the Old Capitol grounds. The state of Illinois also maintains the Lincoln-Herndon law offices across Adams Street. Renovated by private owners in 1968, this building on the south side of the public square was built by Springfield merchant Seth Tinsley in the early 1840s. Abraham Lincoln and law partner William H. Herndon maintained an office there from 1844-1852. Lincoln & Herndon's office has been recreated, as have a post office and federal courtroom, original to the building. The law offices became a state historic site in 1985.

When Lincoln left Springfield in 1861, never to return alive, he delivered a moving farewell speech to friends and well-wishers from the rear of a train car at the city's Great Western Railroad depot, 10th and Monroe streets. In his address, Lincoln expressed his deep regard for Springfield and its residents. That depot has been restored and opened to the public. A recent renovation has been completed by the current owner, Copley Press Incorporated, publishers of *The State Journal-Register* newspaper.

Prior to moving to Springfield in 1837, Abraham Lincoln lived in a small village located near the banks of the Sangamon River—New Salem, now a twenty-minute drive. It was during his New Salem years that Lincoln developed his political and leadership skills. The village existed for only a few years before being abandoned and eventually fell into ruin. As early as 1919 efforts were made to recreate the village. By the 1930s, construction of the first cabins had begun. The state of Illinois maintains the site complete with visitors center, costumed interpreters, and historical gardens and craft demonstrators. Today visitors can stroll down New Salem's one street towards the Sangamon River, past log homes and stores and talk with "residents" of the village going about their daily business.

Springfield's Lincoln connection will be further enhanced with the construction of the Abraham Lincoln Presidential Library. With the help of federal, state, and local government funds, plus private donations, this new presidential center will serve as a starting point for people looking for Lincoln. Everyone from novice to scholar will find an enriched understanding of this venerated American president, thru the library's collections, displays, and interactive exhibits. The Illinois State Historical Library's internationally known Lincoln collection will form the core of the new library's holdings. The historical library has the largest collection of publicly held Lincoln documents in the world.

"If you visit Springfield, Illinois" said *New Yorker* Magazine writer A.J. Liebling in a droll understatement in 1950, "you are bound to get mixed up with Abraham

Attorney Abraham Lincoln and his partner William Herndon had their law offices in this building on the public square. Privately purchased and restored by six preservation-minded Springfieldians in the late 1960s, the Tinsley Building, as it is officially known, became a state historic site in 1986. The building also once housed the post office, federal courtroom, and clerk of the court. It is open to the public and gives a sense of life in 1850 Springfield. Photo by Terry Farmer

Lincoln." It was not only the reverent and serious study of Lincoln, he observed, but the loveable, human quality of locals that put the legendary name on just about any and every kind of enterprise. He found the phonebook chock-full:

...A. Lincoln Tourist Court, the Abe Lincoln Baggage Transfer, the Abraham Lincoln Association...Lincoln Automotive Mechanics School, Lincoln Baggage Transfer Company, Lincoln Cab Company, Lincoln Café, Lincoln Candy Company, Lincoln Cash Market, Lincoln College of Law, Lincoln Dental Laboratories, Lincoln Library...

Well, you get the idea. We suspect that it was Springfieldians' naive, homey, and sincere sense of intimacy with the human Lincoln, the man behind the legend revered around the world, that charmed Liebling and left him to smile over the fact that "nothing, apparently, had been named for Mrs. Lincoln." Today, still, if you visit or live in Springfield, Illinois you are bound to get mixed up with Abraham Lincoln.

Hundreds of thousands of people passing the large bust of Lincoln outside his tomb in Oak Ridge Cemetery have paused to rub his nose for good luck. The local tradition was thought disrespectful by some officials who had the statue raised out of reach. Popular protest brought it back down, something of which, no doubt, the humor-loving Lincoln would have approved. Photo by Terry Farmer

(right) The ghost of Abraham Lincoln still walking at midnight is an image immortalized in the words of renowned poet (and Springfield native) Vachel Lindsay. In fact, several Lincolns still inhabit or visit the town in the personages of numerous impersonators. Photo by Terry Farmer

(opposite) In life Abraham Lincoln expressed the desire to be buried in Springfield's peaceful and beautiful Oak Ridge Cemetery. Today his body rests in an impressively dignified monument in the quietude of the cemetery. Over 400,000 visitors come to pay homage annually. During the 1899-1900 reconstruction, the tomb's obelisk was raised to 117 feet and today towers over the rest of the cemetery. Photo by Terry Farmer

Springfield 25

chapter **two**

2

HISTORY

A *costumed interpreter makes her way along a street in historic New Salem near Springfield. The recreated village documents the 1830s when young Abraham Lincoln was a resident. Photo by Terry Farmer*

Monroe Street at 5th circa 1925. Springfield's downtown was a bustling place in the 1920s. Transportation choices included trolley, buses, and private automobile. A lion's share of commercial businesses, offices, and professionals were located here. The traffic cop, corner news vendors, and crowds of pedestrians all hurry about their business. The big clock at street level of the Ridgley Bank building, center right, provided the time courtesy of bank officers. Claypool's drug store, at left, had been locally famous as the earlier Dodd's Drug Store—a popular gathering spot. "Meet me at Dodd's Corner" had been a familiar refrain among friends since the 19th Century. Photo courtesy of the Lincoln Library, Sangamon Valley Collection

Commerce and government, two cornerstones of Springfield's economy, have played a role in the city's existence since its founding in 1821. That year, the little settlement was made the temporary county seat of newly formed Sangamon County. A rude log courthouse was erected in a field at about the present northwest corner of Second and Jefferson streets. Springfield commerce was pioneered by Elijah Iles, a young entrepreneur from Kentucky, who opened the first store in Springfield. Several stores, taverns, and groceries followed. When the federal land office opened in November 1823, Iles and two other men, Pascal P. Enos and Thomas Cox, purchased the entire village site. The village name was changed to Calhoun but never caught on and reverted to the original—Springfield. In 1825 Springfield was chosen the permanent county seat and became the place of business and entertainment for people in the surrounding countryside as well.

The expanding county seat was incorporated as a town in 1832, although dreams of river town glory were dashed that year when the steamboat Talisman proved unable to navigate the Sangamon River. Springfield's future prosperity was finally assured when it was named the state capital in 1837. By then the state's first railroad was being developed with Springfield as a central point on the line. Railroads would eventually make the town an important transportation center. In 1837 the Northern Cross Railroad was created to run east from the Illinois

This vintage drug store at Sixth and Capitol streets is just one of many interesting downtown spots to gather for coffee, a snack, to catch up on business, celebrate friendships, or just people-watch. Shoppers, store clerks, politicians, lobbyists, lawyers, shopkeepers, government workers, and countless others meet and mingle at the dozens of downtown eateries through the work week. Photo by Terry Farmer

Springfield's lavish Orpheum Theater was a thunderous confection of marble, terra cotta, crystal, mirrors, and gilding that overwhelmed audiences when it opened in 1927. The gleaming terra cotta exterior was, according to one account, "...but a shell for the internal gorgeousness." It was dubbed nothing less than "a veritable palace" for Springfieldians "living in this work-a-day world" and longing "to tread on marble floors, to sweep grandly down palatial stairs as if we owned them, sink voluptuously into thick, rich rugs, revel in the luxuries of a Queen's boudoir." This gilded fantasy existed for only a short life before being demolished in 1965. Photo courtesy of the Lincoln Library, Sangamon Valley Collection

River, pass through Springfield, and reach the borderline with Indiana. Progress on the railroad was slow and it did not reach Springfield until February 15, 1842, and after grimly slow progress, Springfield became a major rail-connecting point.

Springfield became a fully urbanized town during the 1850s and one which grew rapidly as well. The 5,100 people of 1850 became over 9,000 by the decade's end. A public school system, police department, public water supply, and fire department all came into existence in that decade as well.

The last stagecoach line had closed in 1860, as railroads became the primary form of transportation. The city spread out in every direction. Streetcars arrived in 1861 and new arrivals coupled with annexation brought the population to 17,364 inhabitants by 1870. Coal mining that began in earnest in the 1870s provided fuel for manufacturing and employment for hundreds. An industrial corridor developed along the city's 10th Street track. Immigrants arrived in large numbers to work for the railroads, mines, and manufacturing, adding to the ethnic diversity of the city's neighborhoods.

In 1900, at the dawn of the new century, over 34,000 people lived in Springfield. At ten square miles, the town was large enough to have distinctive neighborhoods, many with their own nicknames—Goosetown, Southtown, Vinegar Hill, the North End, Rabbit Row, and Aristocracy Hill, to name just a few. There were 200 miles of streets and a recently electrified streetcar system.

The city also boasted 320 manufacturing establishments, five banks, 10 private schools, 46 churches, three hospitals, two orphanages, a new Illinois State Fairgrounds, City Hall, and brand new public park system. But in contrast to a boosterish pride, there was a more sinister side to life in Springfield—its reputation for gambling, vice, prostitution, and political corruption.

Sentiment for political and social reform also gained strength in those early years of the 20th century. A bloody race riot in 1908, in which two residents were murdered and more than 100 injured, caused Springfield painful embarrassment, but led directly to the founding

Pride in ownership shows in the city's numerous renovated homes. From period paint colors to antique garden flowers, many families have lovingly brought an old house back from neglect and disrepair. The historic Freeman-Hughes House on West Monroe Street is a stunning example. Photo by Terry Farmer

Monroe Street facing east at 5th Street circa 1936. Although the Old Capitol square is the undisputed center of town, Monroe Street runs a close second. In the mid 19th Century, churches lined the corners of Monroe at 2nd, 4th, 5th, 6th, and 7th. By the time of this photo the street formed the busy southern boundary of the central business district. The Ridgley Bank "skyscraper" (top, right) *and the sprawling Bressmer Department Store* (top, left) *dominate the scene. The Senate, Springfield's last downtown theater when it closed in 1983, stands in the center on the left side of the street. Photo courtesy of the Lincoln Library, Sangamon Valley Collection*

Local residents jam the old Chicago and Alton depot at 3rd and Washington streets during World War I. Thousands of departing and returning service men (and women) passed through this station and, when Abraham Lincoln's body made its long journey back from Washington D.C., his funeral train ended here. The present station, built in 1896 and remodeled in 1947, continues to greet arriving and departing passengers who travel AMTRAK. Photo courtesy of the Lincoln Library, Sangamon Valley Collection

"By combining the latest technology with home-grown values and leadership, Brandt Consolidated helps farmers have abundant crops year after year. Brandt Consolidated uses its wealth of knowledge and experience to provide farmers with the best advice and solutions to all their agricultural decisions. Through its retail, dealer support, and ClawEl divisions, it is a leader in today's agricultural business. Most of our business is in the rural communities where we may be the largest employer in that town. Helping our customers produce abundant, high quality crops, and doing it profitably, has driven our company since its inception."

Rick Brandt
President/CEO
Brandt Consolidated, Inc.

(above) *I*nterpreters at New Salem go about everyday tasks with such ease that the pioneer village comes alive for the thousands of visitors who tour it each year. Photo by Terry Farmer

(below) *T*he Lincoln Home National Historic District is the scene of all manner of historical recreations. Here 18th century soldiers perform for audiences recalling 19th century patriotic assemblies that memorialized a romanticized colonial past. Photo by Terry Farmer

The Frank Lloyd Wright-designed Dana-Thomas House comes alive each Christmas season with glowing luminaries and turn-of-the-century Christmas decorations. Photo by Terry Farmer

(opposite) The handsome 1850s Italianate-style headquarters of the Springfield Art Association was long home to the Edwards family. Prominent in state politics, the Edwards were Abraham Lincoln's in-laws and social leaders in polite society in antebellum Springfield. Today the restored home is open to the public. Photo by Terry Farmer

of the National Association for the Advancement of Colored People. A reaction and desire for civic clean-up set in almost immediately. The colorful, outspoken, and entertaining temperance crusader Billy Sunday hosted a weeklong crusade where audiences felt Sunday's outrage against sloth, vice, and the general wickedness of their hometown. Community leaders promoted a change of government, penal, education, and public health reforms. Citizens, in a burst of reform enthusiasm, even voted to outlaw liquor sales in 1917—two years before the National Prohibition Act.

Nineteen-twenties Springfield was marked by prosperity and optimism. A grand city plan was adopted designed to change the face of the city. Despite the Great Depression of the '30s, Lake Springfield (called for in the city plan) was completed. But material shortage during World War II and deferred maintenance during the depression of the 1930s meant the town again became physically shabby. And its civic morals took a beating as well as vice and corruption returned. "Blossomed like the Rose" according to the Saturday Evening Post. But reform again appeared in the 1950s. A movement for better schools and money to pay for them, improved water quality, better police, and fire protection aroused public interest. But it was a crack down on gambling and vice that captured citizen's imagination and gave Springfield a nationwide reputation of improving its civic morals. This second wave of reform and physical clean up had been so far reaching that Springfield was nationally recognized with an All America City designation in 1970.

Springfield over the next generation reflected most of the growth trends of American cities. The central business district, once the primary retail/professional entertainment district, has decentralized. Physically Springfield has expanded to over 60 square miles and retail, entertainment, commercial, and housing development has shifted in large part to the far west edge. This typical suburbanization pattern has actually been taking place since the advent of the streetcars in the 19th Century, but became most evident in the last generation.

A growing interest in preservation and restoration of older neighborhoods and commercial buildings is evident as well. Downtown Springfield Incorporated and other private and public organizations and individuals have been responsible for downtown building façade restorations. Residents of Springfield's Harvard Park are preserving and redeveloping those and other historic city neighborhoods. This past, present, and future is evident. ∫

Springfield 33

chapter | three

3

A CAPITAL ATTRACTION

The state seal of Illinois forms the centerpiece of a magnificent stained glass design towering over the rotunda of the Capitol. The designer of the seal stubbornly placed "State Sovereignty" above "National Union" despite instructions to the contrary. The rogue design remains to this day. Photo by Terry Farmer

The domes of the old and new capitols define the downtown city skyline. The Old State Capitol served as the Sangamon County Courthouse from 1876 to 1965, when it underwent complete demolition and rebuilding to recreate the building as Lincoln knew it. The grand "new" capitol, begun in 1868, took over 20 years to complete. Photo by Terry Farmer

Costumed interpreters welcome guests to the Old State Capitol at the center of Springfield's public square. Candlelight tours recall an evening entertainment as Abraham Lincoln might have known it. Photo by Terry Farmer

Springfield serves as the political nerve center for the state of Illinois. Here the state is governed: legislation debated, laws created, and regulations enforced affecting every resident from Chicago to Cairo. Thousands of state employees—a veritable hive of workers—conduct the endless business of state government. Regulating business, insurance, and commerce, licensing hundreds of thousands of motorists, administering elections, protecting public health, and setting transportation policy are some few of the endless tasks of running Illinois government.

Politics and government—state, federal, and local—are the lifeblood of Springfield and have been so from its beginning. Political logrolling and skillful negotiation by local citizens and their representatives in the Illinois General Assembly won Springfield selection as Illinois' third capital in 1837. Savvy residents offered the added inducement of a public square and a pledge of $50,000 to cover the costs of the removal of government offices from Vandalia, the former capital. The intangible idea of government is expressed in Springfield's state government buildings. Nearly all are suitably grand and each built to impress. The first, the new State House of 1837 is a handsome Greek-Revival-style building designed by John Rague, a Springfield baker and part-time architect, and took until 1853 to complete. The new building, now the Old State Capitol, initially housed all of state offices from Governor to Treasurer. But, as might be expected, in a few short years, exponential government growth resulted in a Capitol bursting at the seams. Nearby office space was rented to handle the overflow.

The new resident governor occupied a house at the northeast corner of Eighth and Capitol (then Market) streets. Stylish and rich, Governor Joel Matteson (1853-1857) found these quarters to be embarrassingly inadequate and pushed thru construction of a new governor's mansion in 1856. This house, at the edge of the Capitol Complex, is still in use today and is the oldest continuously occupied governor's mansion in the country. Several generations of governors walked from this house at Fifth and Jackson streets to their office in the Capitol and it was once the center of a desirable residential neighborhood known as Aristocracy Hill.

A new State House to replace the old, overcrowded Capitol was begun in 1868. The Mather Grove, a tract of land at the southwest corner of Second and Monroe streets, was selected as the site for the structure. A cornerstone laying ceremony was held on October 5, 1868 and it would take nearly 20 years to complete this magnificent temple of government. Beginning about 1900, a complex of related buildings began to rise around it.

In 1902, the first of these was a new state armory at the northwest corner of Second and Monroe streets built to replace the state's first armory of 1855 on North Fifth Street. This second armory, a magnificent Romanesque Revival structure, went up in flames in 1934 at the hands of a child arsonist. Its replacement, on the same site, today houses divisions of the Illinois State Police, though ground is soon to be broken for a new $50 million State Police headquarters immediately west of the Armory.

In 1906 the state purchased the Prickett family property at the southeast corner of Second and Capitol streets as a site for construction of the Illinois Supreme Court Building of 1908. Plans were laid as early as 1915 for an elaborate celebration commemorating the 100th anniversary of Illinois' entry into the union. Over 100 special committees were organized. The Capitol Grounds Purchase Association bought land surrounding the Capitol for planned development of a great complex of neoclassical buildings similar to the Illinois Supreme Court Building. The first building constructed was the Centennial, now the Michael J. Howlett Building, just south of the Capitol. Its first section was quickly finished but it took until 1968 to complete the entire-block square structure. The Illinois State Archives (now Margaret Cross Norton Building) was completed in 1938. In the 1950s and '60s, the Stratton office building and the Illinois State Museum were added to the complex. The much maligned Stratton, ("state workers, I am told, covet offices in it so they won't have to stare at it through their office windows," commented one local wag,) was the first building on the grounds in the self-consciously "modern" International style. In form, though, it retains the formal, symmetrical balance of its earlier neighbors. The Illinois State Library at Second and Capitol was opened in 1990. Renovation work at the former Waterways building for the Fourth District Appellate Court added this formerly private structure to the growing number of state buildings. The Capitol Complex, with the Statehouse as its centerpiece and its collection of official and quasi-official office buildings and parking lots, forms almost a city-within-a-city in near downtown—geographically and culturally dominating Springfield. The state also leases or

*H*ome to Illinois governors since 1855, the Illinois Executive Mansion in downtown Springfield is among the oldest continuously occupied governors' mansions in the country. The house is set on a slight rise of ground and, in the 19th century, was once surrounded by elaborate mansions. When it was built the surrounding neighborhood, in mixed admiration and envy, was dubbed "Aristocracy Hill."
Photo by Terry Farmer

*T*he impressive colonnade of the Illinois Supreme Court Building, with its Beaux Arts-inspired statuary, is an impressive sight on Capitol Avenue. Handsome murals and allegorical figures are a prominent feature of the courtrooms. The 1908 building has recently undergone extensive renovation.
Photo by Terry Farmer

Illinois' present Capitol towers above the Capitol Complex and is a symbol for government and politics that set the stage for so much of Springfield life. A popular subject in all seasons, photographers seem especially to like its aspect in winter. Photo by Terry Farmer

owns numerous other buildings downtown and throughout the city, ranging from the Illinois State Fairgrounds on the north to the McFarland Mental Health Center on the south.

The state of Illinois has over 21,000 employees in Sangamon County alone, making it the area's single largest employer. The Illinois National Guard at Camp Lincoln employs an additional 2,700 people. Offices of federal, county, township, and special district governments also have a local presence. Branches of United States departments from Agriculture, Soil Conservation Service, Army and Air Force recruiting offices, Federal Courts, and Post Office to the Social Security Administration, Federal Aviation Administration, Small Business Administration, and Veterans Clinic are headquartered in Springfield employing hundreds of area people. County government, beginning with Charles Matheny who in 1821 performed all the duties of the county government by himself, has grown to a large network of agencies responsible for zoning, comprehensive planning, public health, highways, real estate ownership, court, and other duties. The $40 million, seven-story county courthouse just east of the Municipal Complex is home to most county agencies. From the 1820s until today the impact of state, federal, county, and township government on the economy of Springfield has been incalculable—truly a capital attraction. ✧

The impressive architecture of the Capitol continues inside the building. House (above) *and Senate* (below) *chambers feature elaborately designed, painted-and-gilded ceilings. Truly stunning public spaces like these are becoming a rarity. Photos by Terry Farmer*

(below) **T**he red stone Sangamon County Complex is an office building housing the multiplicity of county functions from building and zoning through public health and urban planning. Photo by Terry Farmer

(below) **S**tate government buildings extend far beyond the Capitol Complex in downtown Springfield. They are present in all parts of the city. The Illinois Department of Transportation's headquarters overlook a public lake sculpted in the shape of the State of Illinois. Photo by Terry Farmer

(right) **T**he grand architectural quality of the state Capitol is evident throughout its interior. This backdrop in the House Chamber is nearly the size of a small temple itself. The building has been the official symbol of Illinois for nearly a century-and-a-half. Photo by Terry Farmer

(left) **U**nder the magnificent dome of the Illinois capitol visitors mingle with politicians, lobbyists, and those seeking political favors in the colorful, rough-and-tumble world of Illinois politics. The building, constructed in the late 19th century with only horse and manpower, remains an awe-inspiring symbol into the 21st century. Photo by Terry Farmer

(below) **T**he classically inspired grand stairway of the Illinois Executive Mansion, with its delicate balustrade, provides an impressive and elegant background for state functions and entertainments. Photo by Terry Farmer

Springfield 43

chapter | four

4

CENTRAL SUCCESS

Despite Springfield's reputation as a white-collar town where information is the main product, a surprising amount of manufacturing takes place. With products ranging from donuts to mattresses, electronic components to plastics, manufacturing plays an important role in Springfield's robust economy. Photo by Terry Farmer

The land forms the basis of central Illinois' great wealth and despite technological advances, development of agri-business and bio-engineering, the basic miracle of the growing cycle remains unchanged, season after season, year upon year.
Photo by Terry Farmer

Nestled amidst some of the richest farmland in the world, Springfield has always benefited directly from agricultural wealth, particularly in its early days as a market and trading town. From this agrarian base Springfield developed a robust and diverse economy in the last century-and-a-half that, in addition to agriculture, has come to include banking, insurance, retail business, manufacturing, technology, medical care, government, tourism, and even printing and publishing. From the first days local citizens expressed entrepreneurial energy and a spirit of pragmatic problem solving that made for success, even in the face of adversity. The first major hurdle, a lack of dependable, efficient transportation, was overcome with promotion of railroads in the 1840s. From that day forward Springfield began its steady growth from primitive settlement to county seat to capital of a major industrial state. Transportation and communication technology—railroads, interurbans, automobiles and telegraph, telephone, and internet—have all played a part in keeping Springfield connected nationally and internationally for business, entertainment, information, and commerce.

But it was agriculture that gave the community its first economic advantage. Lacking hard cash, many farmers bartered crops and livestock with city merchants in order to get the supplies they needed. Springfield's business revolved around agriculture. Flour and carding mills processed wheat and wool while businessmen like James L. Lamb opened a pork packing firm important throughout the region. Foundries opened for the manufacture of

A bright, curious fowl looks back at the camera from her perch at the Illinois State Fair. The fair began in the 1850s as an agricultural education enterprise reflecting Illinois' agrarian culture. Today it is a major entertainment attraction for the city and central Illinois.
Photo by Terry Farmer

Energy, *the basis for smooth-running commerce, business, and manufacturing, is plentiful in Springfield. The city-owned municipal power plant burns Illinois coal, scrubbed clean after combustion. Photo by Terry Farmer*

wagons, plows, and other implements for use by farmers. Clearly the entire economy was once agriculture-dependant.

But manufacturing and industry, coupled with an enviable system of railroad transportation by the late 1800s, produced truly fabulous riches for the community. Government contracts during the Civil War pushed local companies into new and more rapid methods of production and set the stage for a wave of industrialism in the late 19th century. New manufacturers and industries ranged from a watch factory to iron mills, shoe manufacturer and electric meter maker, all fueled by the seemingly limitless reserves of coal discovered in the area and mined by thousands of men and boys. By the Great Depression of the 1930s, as coal mining and great numbers manufacturing jobs decreased, growth of state government assured economic stability. Today's complex economy includes a more dominant role played by banking and insurance as well. Many Springfield banks had their origins over a hundred years ago. The first bank in Springfield, the Illinois State Bank, was established in 1835. It proved a failure and closed in 1842. Springfield residents then turned to trustworthy merchants like Jacob Bunn and John Williams to hold their money in store safes. Both Bunn and Williams moved on to careers as bankers. Springfield Marine and Fire Insurance (an insurance company with banking privileges) was chartered in 1851. Springfield Marine and Fire still exists today as Bank One. John Williams organized the First National Bank (today's Firstar) in 1863 as a successor to his private bank. National City Bank, originally known as Illinois National Bank, was organized in 1886.

Springfield's *architectural community is kept busy with numerous private and public projects underway each year. Photo by Terry Farmer*

Springfield is a community of neighborhoods. In contrast to the new suburbs of the far west side, are the dozens of historic neighborhoods closer to the central city. There are many blocks of well-kept, older homes along streets lined with mature trees. This attractive cottage typifies the appeal of those neighborhoods that charm many homebuyers. Photo by Terry Farmer

New institutions have recently revived the Illinois National Bank and Marine names. The banking industry has increased heavily in Springfield with many neighboring community banks opening branches in Springfield. Today there are over 15 banks in the Springfield area, employing hundreds of persons.

Insurance companies and their representatives also played an early role in Springfield. The Sangamon Insurance Company opened for business in Springfield in 1857. Locally, companies like American General Financial Group had their beginnings in the 1800s as well. Several Springfield businessmen organized Franklin Life Insurance, the ancestor of American General, in 1881. The Franklin, which was sold in 1995, grew to become a major Springfield employer. Springfield educators Carroll C. Hall and Leslie W. Nimmo co-founded Horace Mann Insurance Company in 1945. Encompassing two downtown city blocks, Horace Mann's headquarters were constructed in 1969.

Signaled by the opening of White Oaks Mall in the 1970s, Springfield has enjoyed a new and continually growing role as a regional retail and service center in the last 30 years. As the city expands physically, outward, so does Springfield's retailing impact. In many ways it is again a major economic locus for central Illinois, much like the 1830s and '40s when Springfield was the market town for the surrounding territory.

Construction and engineering firms are in constant demand in a rapidly expanding city. General contractors and those specializing in electrical, excavating, heating, or plumbing work, are numerous, as well as those doing highway and heavy construction.

The city's infrastructure is in a constant state of building and rebuilding, including roads, communication channels—from telephone to fiber optics—and water, sewer, and electrical lines.

Although a smaller part of the economic picture than in the 19th century, manufacturing still plays an important role. In addition to traditional products like mattresses and automobile components, more unusual items, from a world-famous coffee maker to mortar coloring used in construction projects across the nation, are made here. Springfield firms produce a wide variety of goods including airline parts, chemicals, electrical fittings, food items,

Medical technology plays a large role in the Springfield economy. Photo by Terry Farmer

Central Illinois' landscape of corn and soybean fields is punctuated by grazing meadows and undulating groves of trees. This bucolic scene is typical of the countryside around Springfield. Photo by Terry Farmer

Springfield Mass Transit District buses carry residents to their destinations daily including many state of Illinois and downtown workers. Few riders are likely aware that many route line names like "Country Club" and "Monroe Street" derive from the old street car lines that once criss-crossed the town. Photo by Terry Farmer

construction products, and, increasingly, high-technology items including computer software and hardware.

And, significantly, a large amount of businesses exist whose product is service or information—public relations firms, personnel services, landscapers, personal shoppers, and fitness trainers, software programmers and designers, architects, engineers, product researchers, limousine services, shipping and mailing providers, commercial cleaning companies, realtors—the list is endless. This sometimes overlooked sector provides almost a quarter of the jobs in the Springfield area.

All of these manufacturers, retailers, service, insurance, banking, and other businesses are linked together to form the complex web that makes up the local economy. Economic development has been the main Springfield theme over the last generation. The Springfield area, based on its historic success, will certainly continue to thrive and prosper no matter what changes of emphasis take place in the economy, in business, transportation, communication, or services. From the opening of town founder Elijah Iles' first trading store in 1821 to today's retailing center, Springfield exemplifies the spirit of entrepreneurial adventure and chance-taking identified with economic success. *S*

A present day "trolley ride" takes visitors to local historic sites like the Frank Lloyd Wright-designed Dana-Thomas House shown here. Photo by Terry Farmer

High tech applications appear in the most surprising places in Springfield—like donut making. Mel-O-Cream is a famous local business that has been producing tempting American favorites since 1932. A product line of the familiar "O" with a hole runs past the inspector's eye. Photo by Terry Farmer

"**P**eople, the right people, are a company's greatest source of profitability and Express is helping companies secure those right people. We have become the way that companies acquire their workforce and the way that people go to work. Our vision statement sums up our dedication to the Springfield community: To help as many people as possible find good jobs by helping as many clients as possible find good people, and help clients make those jobs and those people even better. This vision enables Express to ensure Springfield remains a central success."

Jim Britton
Franchisee/Regional Developer
Express Personnel Services

(right) **C**apital Airport connects the local community with the outside world. Arriving legislators, departing manufacturers seeking new markets, and the vacationing public pass through its terminal. Railroad, shuttle, and bus facilities also offer travel options. Photo by Terry Farmer

(below) **T**he oldest newspaper in Illinois, The State Journal-Register is published from this complex at 9th and Monroe streets. Photo by Terry Farmer

Springfield is a town full of hobby/recreation organizations. A fan of antique autos plans a route to follow in his open touring car. Antique automobile meets and shows are popular with collectors and public alike. Photo by Terry Farmer

Photo by Terry Farmer

Springfield 55

chapter **five**

5

EDUCATIONAL EXCELLENCE

Educational excellence is a high priority in Springfield. School choices range from a public school system, inaugurated in 1850, through an array of private schools and academies, public and private colleges, and universities. Photo by Terry Farmer

The future of a community lies in its children and Springfield youngsters have a rich variety of educational and recreational offerings. Photo by Terry Farmer

Starting with its first subscription schools in the 1820s, Springfield has long made a commitment of educating its young people. A number of private academies and tutors instructed the children of the city until free public education was made available in the mid-19th century. Today the city boasts a fine public school system, several denominational schools, and colleges and universities.

The Springfield public school system began in 1854 with four elementary or "ward" schools—one in each of the city's four political wards. The first public high school opened in 1857. Population growth resulted in the establishment of more public schools to meet the needs of educating additional children. Middle schools, first developed in the 1930s, took a strong hold in the 1950s. Edison, Jefferson, and Grant middle schools all opened in that decade. Feitshans and Lanphier joined Springfield's first high school in the 1930s. Feitshans was replaced by Southeast High School in 1967. The school district currently has over 14,000 students enrolled. The Capital Area Career Center, located near the University of Illinois at Springfield, provides vocational training to over 800 students in 17 career fields including agriculture, communications, health occupations, and law enforcement. Communications and media students gain useful skills in the school's radio station, WQNA-FM and television studios. Recent developments in education including charter and year-round curriculum are being tested at some public schools in the city. Despite the

The invention of the computer and its related technology have changed the world, arguably, even more than landing on the moon. Springfield's newest citizens form the first generation who never knew life without computers. Integration of this technology into local classroom instruction assures that students master the skills they need in this challenging new world. Photo by Terry Farmer

challenge of growing suburban districts drawing away families and a consequent decline in student population, Springfield public schools have maintained an enviable level of academic achievement. The schools are also well-known for their outstanding athletic programs from baseball and golf to soccer and swimming.

Springfield also has a fine tradition of excellent private school education. The first Catholic high school (Ursuline Academy) opened its doors in 1857. Roman Catholic parochial elementary schools were established in 1860 with a small school next to St. Mary's Church. Springfield presently has about 10 Catholic grade schools and two high schools, Ursuline and Sacred Heart-Griffin. The Lutheran Church, which began its own school system in the mid-1850s, currently supports four elementary schools and one high school. Other denominational schools include Christian, Baptist, and Pentecostal. Calvary Academy, which is affiliated, with the non-denominational Calvary Chapel offers instruction from elementary through high school. A special private school is the Hope School, which opened in 1957. Hope's mission is to serve and educate children with multiple disabilities.

Complementing Springfield's primary education system is a mixture of private and public universities and colleges. Historically the city has excelled in educational opportunities. The first institution for secondary education opened in 1852 as the private Illinois State University which ceased operation in 1867. In 1874 Concordia Theological Seminary occupied the campus after moving from St. Louis. Local citizens were once even able to take advantage of special studies at a law school, a music conservatory, and teachers training school. While higher education existed in 19th century Springfield at Concordia Lutheran Seminary, students were of course limited to those preparing for the ministry. But locals long-dreamed of a university in Springfield. That dream nearly came true in 1924 with the founding of Abraham Lincoln University. The first students had actually been accepted, and land set aside for the campus. But financial shortfalls meant a dream delayed. In the meantime, the

A strong mind and a healthy body is an ideal local educators strive to achieve for the kids in their charge. Play and recreation places abound in the community—on the school ground and off. Photo by Terry Farmer

The impressive Illinois State Library is one of the newest buildings in the Illinois State Capitol Complex. Libraries, cornerstones for lifelong learning, have a large presence in Springfield. In addition to the State Library, there are university and college libraries, an excellent public library system, Supreme Court Library, Legislative Reference Bureau, State Historical Library, and numerous specialized private business libraries. Photo by Terry Farmer

Lincoln Land Community College serves all or parts of 15 surrounding counties from its Springfield campus and regional educational centers. Lincoln Land students are prepared for entry into upper level schools including the University of Illinois at Springfield. Photo by Terry Farmer

Catholic-affiliated Springfield Junior College (today's Springfield College in Illinois) opened in 1929, giving area people their first opportunity for higher education without leaving the city. Today, as Springfield College in Illinois, the school, with about 400 students, offers degrees in several liberal arts fields. The late 1960s witnessed a remarkable period of growth in education. This nationwide trend of increasing public support for education meant the opening of many new schools particularly at the upper level. Springfield gained a community college and university during those years, reflecting this trend. Both schools began in temporary, makeshift quarters but are now housed on beautiful campuses southeast of Springfield.

Lincoln Land Community College, founded in 1968, offers over 40 course areas in its transfer degree program and additional choices in its applied sciences program. The school, whose education district encompasses all or parts of 15 counties, has its main campus in Springfield but also maintains regional education centers in six other communities spread across its district. LLCC's academic program complements its neighboring educational institution, the University of Illinois at Springfield. UIS was founded in 1970 as Sangamon State University. Taking advantage to its proximity to state, federal, and local government, the school was given a mandate for the study of public affairs and government. Now the third campus of the University of Illinois, the institution offers

20 undergraduate majors with an emphasis on public affairs instruction, research, and service. Originally an upper division institution, the university is accepting freshmen students for the first time through its Capital Scholars Program. With an enrollment of 4,000 students, the University of Illinois at Springfield is the largest secondary education institution in the city following Southern Illinois University School of Medicine. UIS' 700-acre campus is located southeast of Springfield.

Southern Illinois University's School of Medicine, which also came to Springfield in 1970 is a prime reason for the city's rise as a medical center and top healthcare provider in central Illinois. This nationally recognized medical school provides students a four-year program and residencies for a number of them afterward. The campus of the medical school is ideally situated near Memorial Medical Center and not far from St. John's Hospital. Both facilities provide valuable learning situations for student physicians.

Besides the university and colleges that offer a wide range of degrees, Springfield is also home to institutions catering to specific career training. Robert Morris

(left) *Founded in 1970, Southern Illinois University's School of Medicine brought a new dimension of medicine and medical research to the community. But the qualities of beauty and meditation are present in the campus alongside the technical and practical. An outdoor sculpture rests in a ring of greenery. Photo by Terry Farmer*

(below) *Online instruction has brought with it a new world of learning. Springfield people have opportunities for study in local classrooms or infinite choices of tutorials from anywhere in the world. Photo by Terry Farmer*

Robert Morris College, the fastest growing private college in Illinois, was originally founded as a junior college in Carthage, Illinois in 1965. It has become an established and contributing institution in the Springfield community focused on educating and preparing students for the world of work in today's rapidly changing corporate environment. An astounding 97 percent of RMC students find jobs upon graduation. Photo by Terry Farmer

College, opened in 1988, offers degrees focused on applied studies in business and allied health. St. John's College at St. John's Hospital is devoted solely to the education of professional nurses. Nursing students are trained with a combination of professional classes and clinical experience after completing two years of lower division college.

Continuing outward growth of Springfield has resulted in several nearby communities becoming a part of the Springfield urbanized area. The villages of Chatham, Rochester, Sherman, and Pleasant Plains are, in many ways, much like Springfield suburbs. The high quality of education provided in these and neighboring communities attract many Springfield-area families.

Springfield's rich educational offerings—from pre-school to post graduate—offer a wide variety of choices in learning for residents. From traditional kindergarten through high school, college, or vocational degrees, and classes for self-improvement or entertainment—the choices are plentiful. It's a truism in the city that for anyone seeking to further their education, "when a teacher is needed, one appears." 𝒮

Springfield 61

The University of Illinois at Springfield campus was founded in 1970 as Sangamon State University. Taking advantage of its location in Springfield, site of so much political and governmental activity—state, federal, and municipal—UIS offers students an emphasis on public affairs and civic improvement. Photo by Terry Farmer

From *The Nutcracker* to *Rockballet*, the Springfield Ballet Company presents diverse, exciting productions. Hard work, determination, and a sense of fun keep the company alive and vital. Photo by Terry Farmer

Community theatre gets great play in Springfield. From student productions to the local Theatre Centre and open-air Municipal Opera on Lake Springfield, audiences and actors share the drama, sweat, and occasional frustration of theater production. Photo by Terry Farmer

The University of Illinois at Springfield brings a wide cultural menu to Springfield including art exhibits like this one in the university's art gallery at left. But sports, concerts, theater, public readings, and professional entertainers are regularly on the bill, filling its athletic fields and the Sangamon Auditorium (below). *Photos by Terry Farmer*

"All great cities must be able to boast of a strong public school system and world-class institutions of higher learning. And all outstanding school systems and world-class colleges and universities exist in part because of the great cities in which they thrive. Springfield and its educational partners have established and nurtured brilliant associations over the years that have benefited thousands of citizens. The fact that the futures of this city and its schools are inextricably linked should bring great satisfaction to all who reside here."

Richard D. Ringeisen
Chancellor
University of Illinois at Springfield

Springfield 65

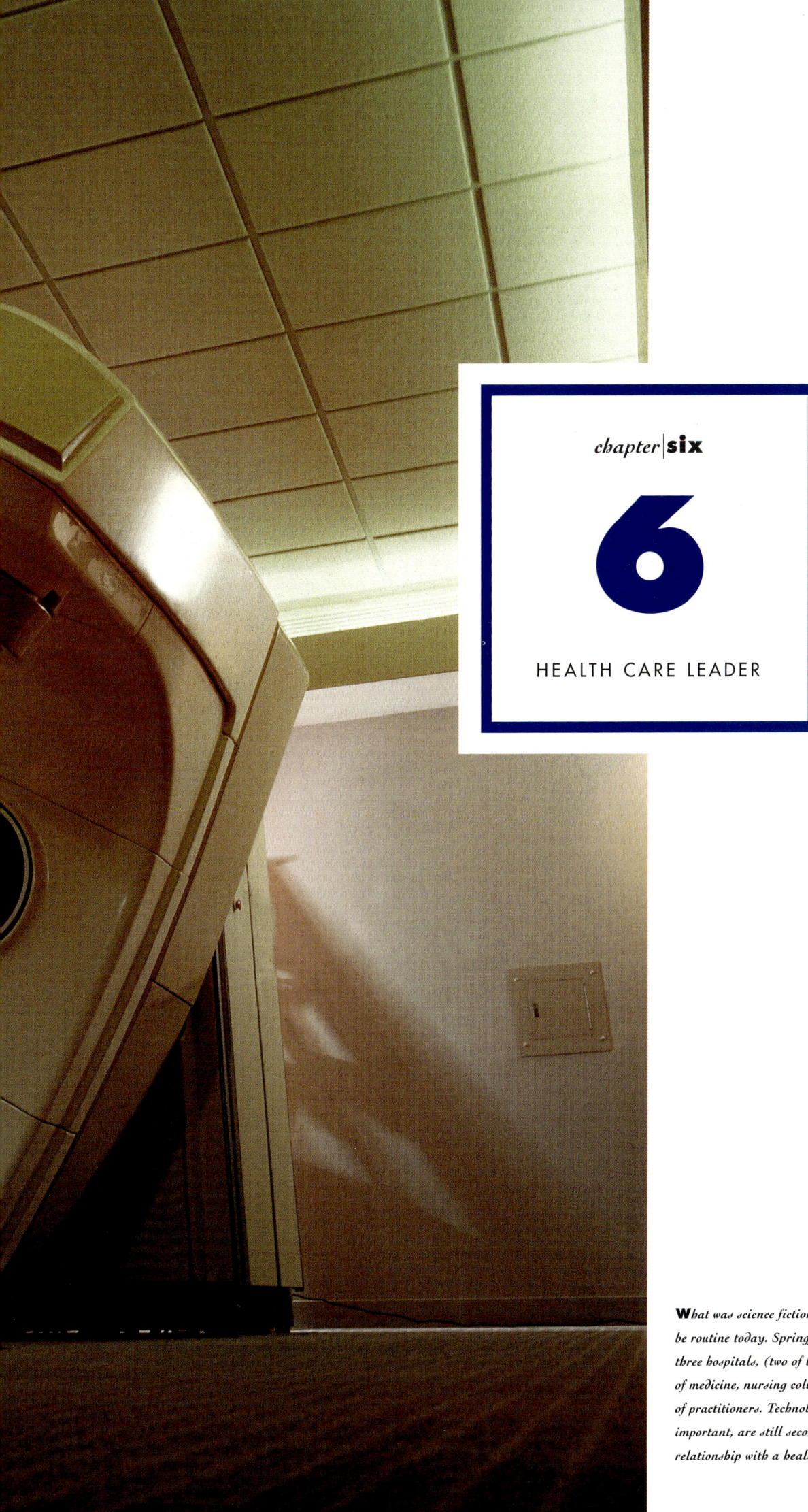

chapter|six

6

HEALTH CARE LEADER

What was science fiction in medicine a generation or so ago can be routine today. Springfield is a regional medical center with three hospitals, (two of them teaching), several clinics, a school of medicine, nursing college, and a widely respected population of practitioners. Technology and equipment, while phenomenally important, are still secondary to a patient's personal, caring relationship with a health care provider. Photo by Terry Farmer

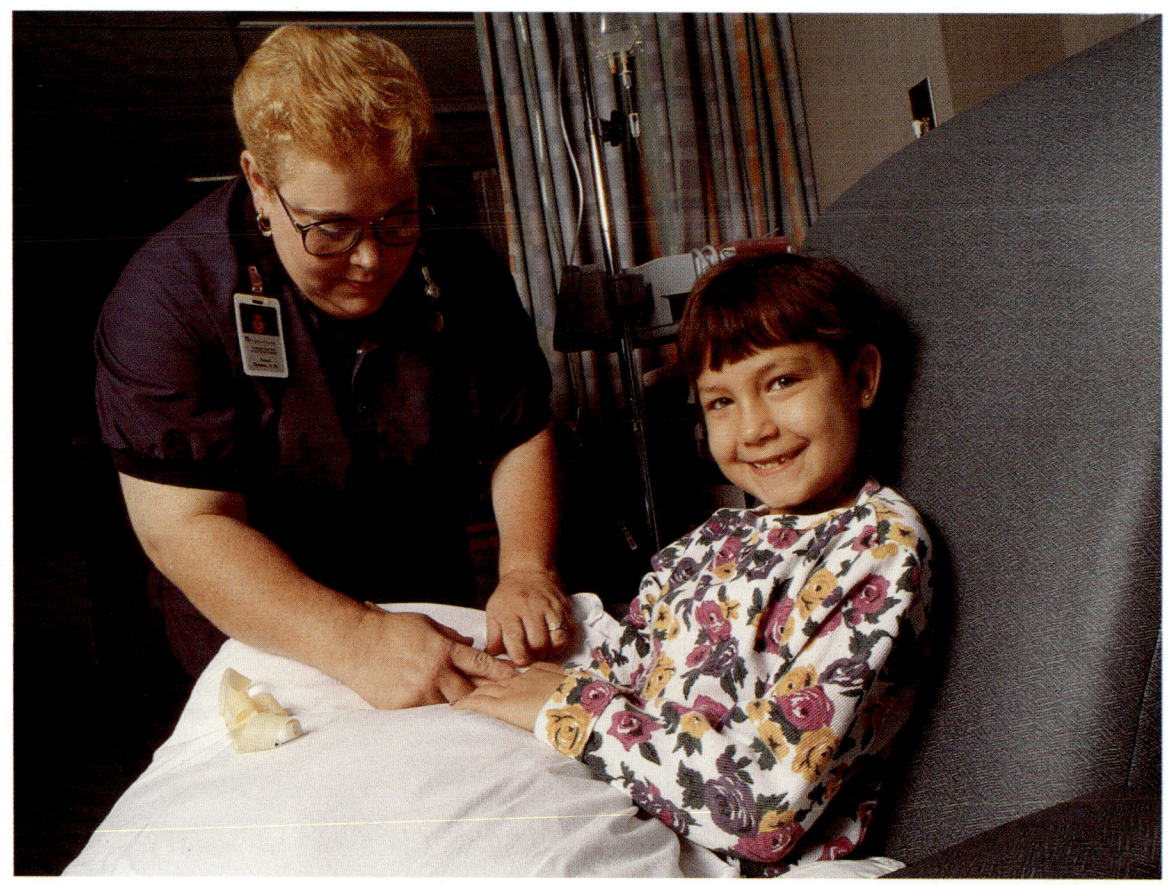

Nursing care and personal attention make all the difference in a hospital stay or through an illness. Springfield healthcare professionals can brighten life for a child coping with illness...
Photo by Terry Farmer

...Or an adult dealing with infirmities or illness of old age. Through a medical network of referrals, families can find support services appropriate to every stage and circumstance in life.
Photo by Terry Farmer

Medical care in Springfield has changed dramatically since Dr. Gershom Jayne hung his shingle up in 1821, becoming the city's first physician. Today health care services form a major sector of the city's economy, second only to government in size—a complex and highly technical maze of hospital systems, clinics, specialists, and group health plans including health maintenance organizations. With its state-of-the-art health care Springfield has become a regional center for Central and Southern Illinois residents requiring specialized care. Regional programs like the Heart Institute at St. John's Hospital and Regional Cancer Center at Memorial Medical Center have earned Springfield a national reputation as a health care provider.

In 19th century Springfield a wide variety of medical practitioners including homoeopathists, eclectic, and other types of physicians, provided medical care for the fast-growing city. Springfield's first hospital, St. John's, was established in 1875. Springfield Hospital and Training School, the ancestor of Memorial Medical Center, was founded in 1897. Other 19th century hospitals included the Wabash Railroad Hospital for railroad employees and David Prince Sanitarium specializing in the eye, ear, nose and throat, and diseases of women.

St. John's Hospital was founded by a group of Hospital Sisters of Saint Francis recently arrived in Springfield from Germany. By living in comparative poverty themselves, the Sisters were able to raise enough funds to build a new hospital at the corner of Eighth and Mason Streets which still remains the site of St John's. The original hospital building went through numerous additions and replacements expanding to eventually cover several square blocks today—a prominent city landmark immediately north of downtown. Some of the outstanding programs at the hospital include the Prairie Heart Institute, Carol Jo Vecchie Women and Children's Center, and the Center for Mind-Body Medicine. The Prairie Heart Institute was created in 1994 as a joint venture between St. John's Hospital and Prairie Cardiovascular Consultants Limited. The Institute is the largest heart program in Illinois, performing more diagnostics catheritizations, angioplasties, and heart surgeries than any other hospital in the region. Family-centered care focusing on children and women is the specialty of the Carol Jo Vecchie Women and Children's Center. The Center is home to the Birth Center, Neonatal Intensive Care Unit, and Women's programs. St. John's employs over 3,500 people.

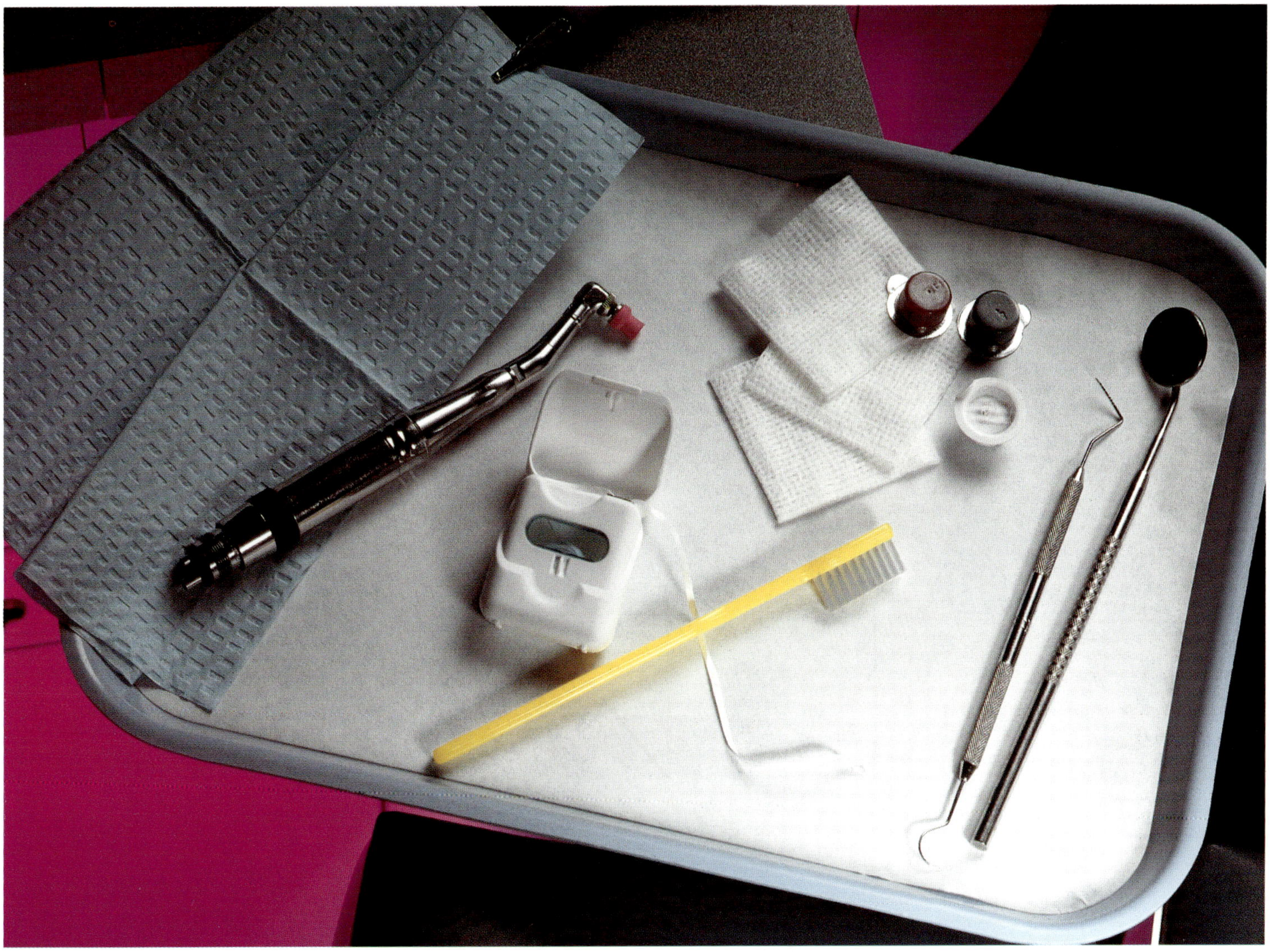

Springfield Hospital and Training School was founded in 1897 under the auspices of the local Lutheran Church aimed specifically at serving the city's non-Catholics. The hospital struggled for many years to remain financially solvent while providing quality health care to the community. The institution changed its name to Memorial Hospital in 1943 reflecting its new emphasis as a community-wide rather than sectarian hospital. Now, as Memorial Medical Center, the hospital is the main link in the chain of health care providers that make up the Memorial Health System. Memorial is an acute care hospital with 500-plus beds and more than 3,500 employees including over 500 physicians, offering comprehensive inpatient and outpatient medical services. Memorial's specialty clinics include the Regional Cancer Center, Regional Burn Center, and Sports Care of Illinois. Memorial recently opened its Koke Mill Medical Center on Springfield's west side housing specialist offices as well as surgical suites, lab, and x-ray facilities.

Once rivals, St. John's and Memorial now collaborate in many types of alliances offering medical care to Springfield residents. One recent effort is the Southern Illinois Trauma Center, which opened in 1999 as a

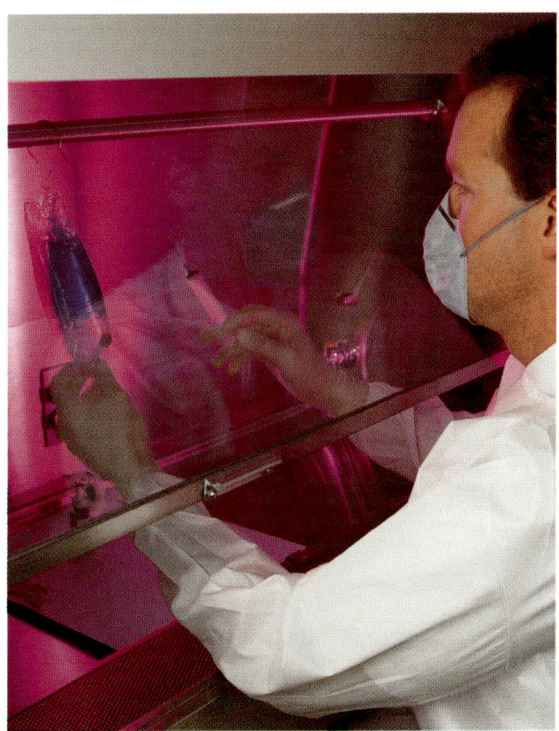

"Painless dentistry," that often-promised but seldom-delivered hope of 19th century dental care, has become almost a reality. The tools of the trade and a visit to the dentist's office inspire so much less trepidation these days. Springfield's dental society, dating back to the early 1900s, continues to promote professional, high quality care and treatment. Photo by Terry Farmer

A small army of medical laboratory workers, in local hospitals and private facilities, supports Springfield's complex of medical care programs. Photo by Terry Farmer

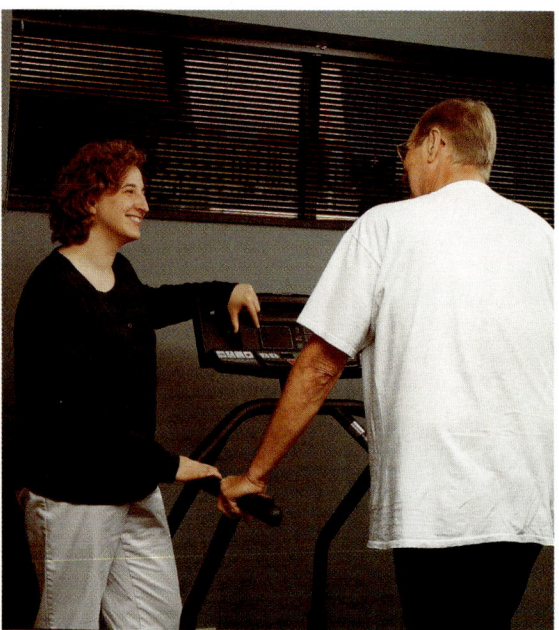

Physical rehabilitation after an accident, illness, or injury is essential for continued health and independence. Rehab programs have made great strides in the city, particularly since the opening of the SIU School of Medicine. The med school, city hospitals, and private agencies offer rehabilitation services from stroke recovery to sports medicine. Photo by Terry Farmer

Medical students in the Springfield community have an outstanding selection for hands-on and observational learning. Hospitals and clinics provide experience not found in the classroom alone. Technological advances including video learning add to a rich learning environment. Photo by Terry Farmer

Medicine has specialized to an incredible degree in the last 50 years. The Chest Pain Center is just one example of that continuing trend. Springfield's reputation throughout the region as a leading medical center has come, in large part, from the level of highly skilled and specialized health care providers. Photo by Terry Farmer

cooperative effort between the two hospitals and Southern Illinois University School of Medicine.

Springfield Clinic, which was born as a business arrangement between five Springfield physicians in 1939, has grown into a medical staff of over 185 physicians and surgeons representing over 30 specialties. The Clinic has facilities located in several Springfield locations and in surrounding counties as well. It is the second largest physicians group in central Illinois.

The newest entrant among health care providers in Springfield, Doctors Hospital, opened its doors in 1975 as part of a growing trend in community medical care. Doctors Hospital is a private, for-profit facility owned by Health Management Limited Partnership. This 177-bed, acute care hospital provides a number of inpatient and outpatient services including medical/surgical care, psychiatric care, and skilled nursing service. The hospital employs approximately 530 people. It is the home to the Central Illinois Eye Institute and Heartland Plastic Surgery Center.

Other health clinics that have opened in recent times include the Capitol Community Health Center and the Veterans Administration Clinic. Capital Community Health Center was created in 1999 with funding received from a federal grant. The Center serves primarily the residents of Springfield's east side but is open to all uninsured residents of Sangamon County. The Veterans Administration opened an outpatient clinic for veterans in 2000. The clinic, in a small medical building, was immediately in high demand by area veterans.

The city's wide-ranging health care providers also include a generous number of dentists; mental health specialists, chiropractors, and growing list of alternative care practitioners. City and county health is monitored by the Springfield and Sangamon County health departments which provide restaurant inspections, vaccinations among other public services. Maintaining a rich, rewarding, and independent life by an aging population is made possible by a wealth of retirement communities, meal delivery, and personal service providers. While not strictly medical in nature, this segment supports the ability of residents to remain active and involved in the community well into traditional "retirement" years. Hospice and end-of-life care in Springfield is outstanding with model programs being affiliated with both hospitals.

The continuing expansion and diversification in the medical care sector by hospitals, clinics, physician groups, and other health care providers has made an enormous impact on the economy of Springfield in the past few decades. Research activities at the hospitals and

70 Springfield

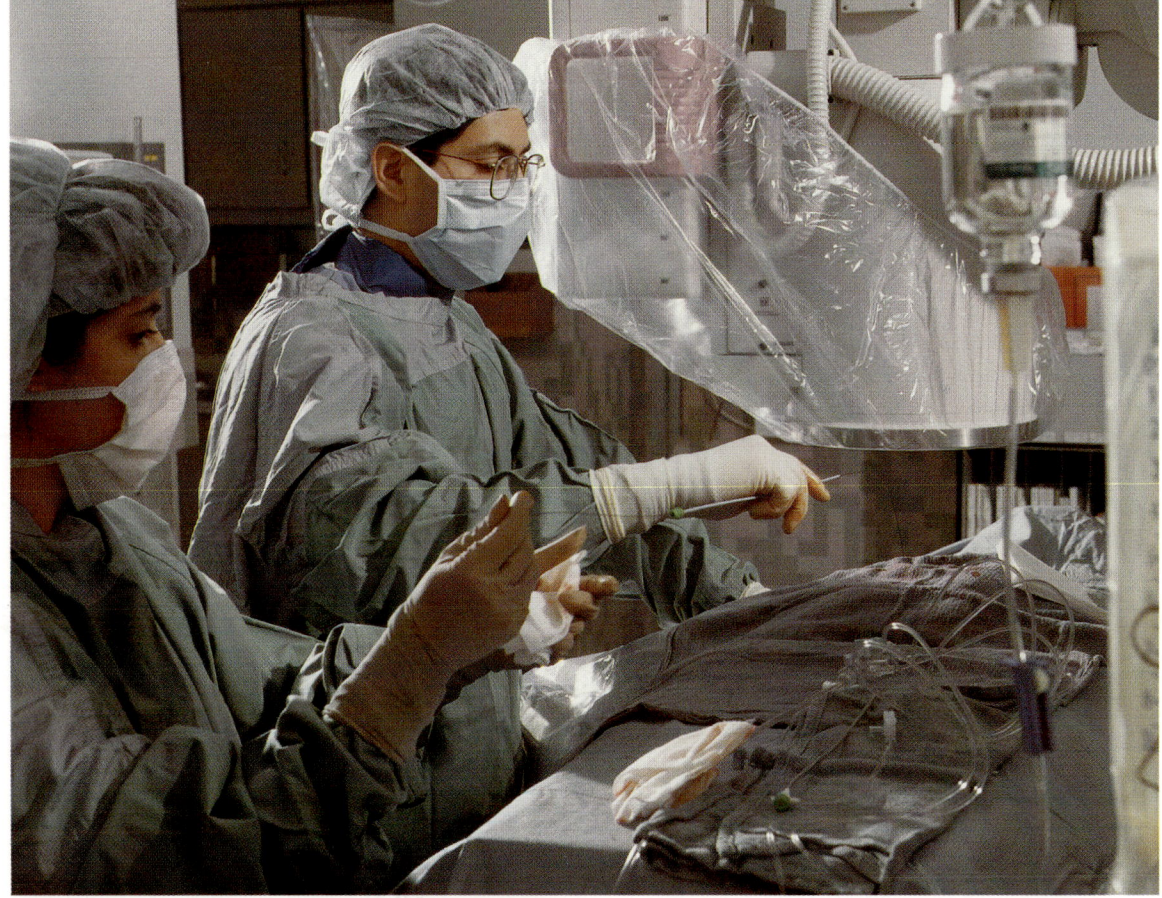

The explosion of medical technology in the last generation is plainly evident in Springfield, which has become a regional medical center. Cutting-edge procedures and equipment usually found in cities many times larger are available here. An entire community of inter-dependent medical staff network in providing top-rated patient care from minor to major.
Photo by Terry Farmer

Medical dramas, large and small, play out every day in the city. From the solitary technician patiently seeking answers (right) to the teamwork required in the operating room with its atmosphere of agonizing and exhilarating suspense (opposite), medicine plays a large role in community life.
Photos by Terry Farmer

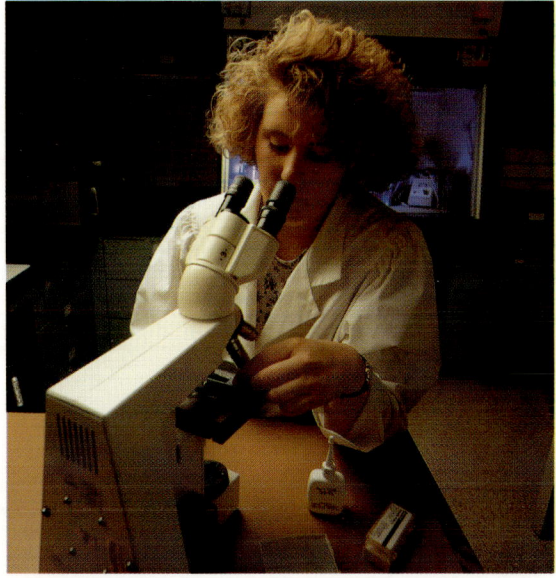

SIU School of Medicine are important to this expansion through adding millions of dollars in funding as well as improving health care in the city through new research and discoveries. The city of Springfield aids in this growth as well by actively promoting the community's excellent health care at trade shows. Four of the ten top employers in Sangamon County are health-care related. Medicine offers both medical and economic vitality to the Springfield community. ℐ

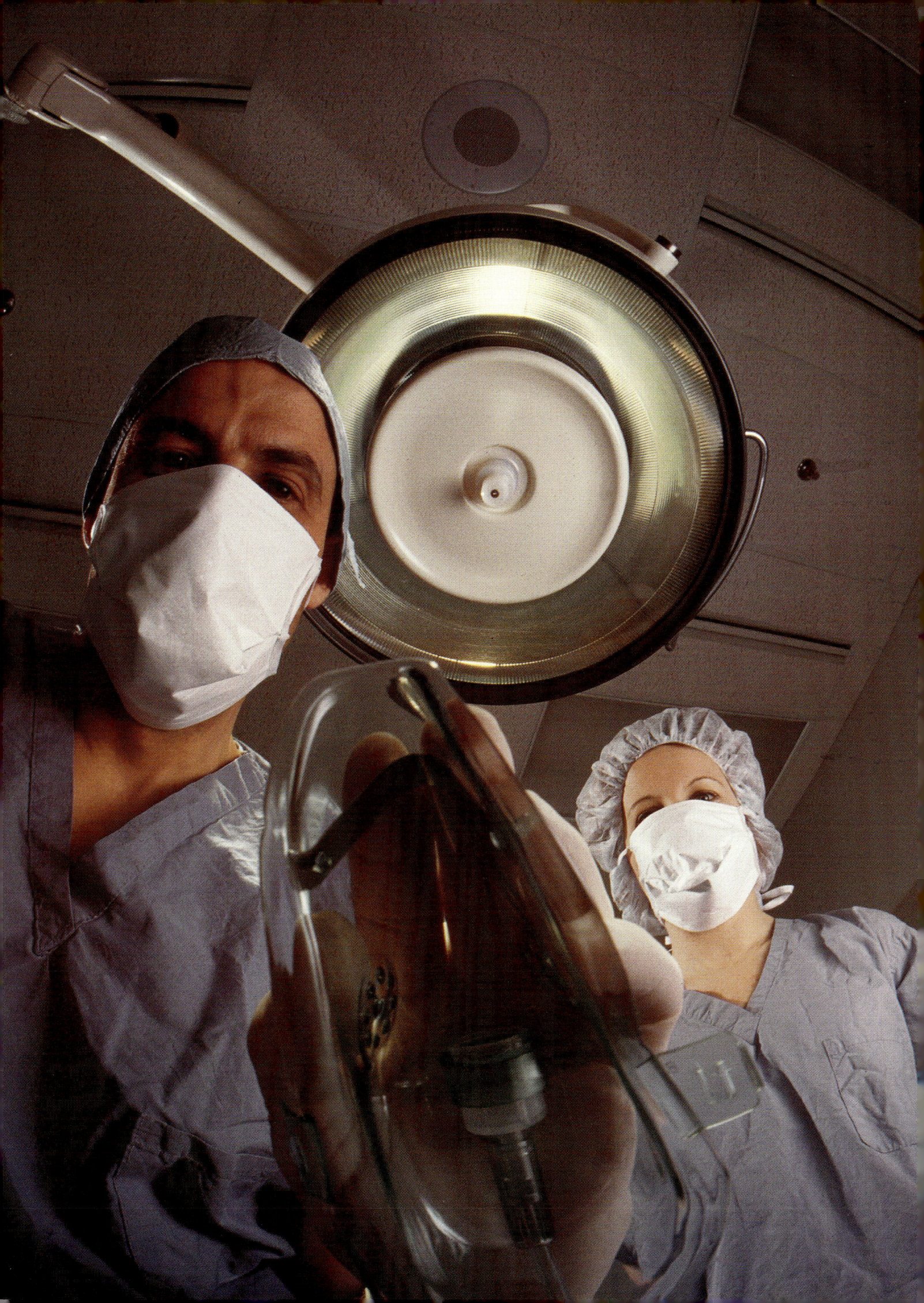

72 Springfield

Not all medical care is of the urgent, high-tech kind. Therapists working one-on-one with a child can make a life-long difference. Springfield has been praised as a caring community and seldom is that more evident than in the relationship between caregiver and patient. Photo by Terry Farmer

Springfield 75

chapter | **seven**

7

THINGS TO SEE AND DO

Recreation has a big role in Springfield life. The locals literally "re-create" themselves when pursuing leisure activities whether jogging or swimming, biking or meditating, reading or cheering their favorite team. From touring local sites and festivals, exploring parks and trails, soaking up the sun to soaking up culture, Springfield has almost limitless ways to fill the relaxing time. Photo by Terry Farmer

(above) *The silhouette of a Ferris Wheel highlighted by an azure Illinois summer sky symbolizes the carefree atmosphere of a day at the fair. The Illinois State Fair has been permanently located in Springfield since 1893. Photo by Terry Farmer*

(above right) *The simple dignity of the Korean War Memorial is perfectly complimented by the quiet beauty of its setting in Oak Ridge Cemetery. Photo by Terry Farmer*

Springfield offers a myriad of activities for every recreational interest—hiking, sporting events, boating, golf, swimming, theater, dance, festivals, fairs, the arts, and so much more. All of these opportunities make a culturally diverse community. Arts and recreation also boost the local economy and add drama and interest to life in the capital.

The city of Springfield has a treasure trove of parks, gardens, trails, and water courses to explore. The Springfield Park District was formed in 1900 and today oversees several parks, scattered throughout the area, that are heavily used for exercise, sports, fishing, and social functions. The Nelson Center, managed by the district, is home to the city's largest public swimming pool and also offers two ice rinks. Washington Park, the first project of the new park district, is a gem of landscape architecture. Designed by nationally-recognized park architect O.C. Simonds, it is an outstanding example of urban park design. Though only 150 acres in size, it appears much larger due to careful layout of roads, wooded screening, and vistas. Lauded for its naturalistic beauty at its 1902 opening, the park was Springfield's premier recreational site—offering facilities for tennis, cycling, rowing, strolling, and carriage riding. Today, except for carriage rides and rowboating, Washington Park still offers these recreational outlets. Washington Park Botanical Gardens, the only one of its kind in central Illinois, and Rees Memorial Carillon are two distinctive features of the park. Washington was joined by Lincoln and Bunn parks and a dozen smaller ones in the century since the Park District's founding. The District now boasts of 37 parks covering a total of over 1600 acres. The newest and largest of the city's parks is Centennial Park on the city's far west side. Henson Robinson Zoo, located near Lake Springfield, is home to more than 33 species of exotic and native animals and attracts 100,000 visitors a year.

Trails for cycling, jogging, and walking are being developed along abandoned railroad rights of ways in the city and many more are planned. Lost Bridge Trail connecting Springfield and the village of Rochester is one of the most popular. Nature lovers can take the trail through the 30-acre Adams Wildlife Sanctuary which is supported by the Illinois Audubon Society. Exhibits of native plants can be viewed along the trails of Lincoln Memorial Garden and Nature Center, was designed by famed landscape architect Jens Jensen.

Besides being the home of the Lincoln Tomb, Oak Ridge Cemetery is the final resting place for most of the city's early residents. The cemetery, designed by prominent landscape designer William Saunders who also created Gettysburg National Cemetery, is the resting place of three Illinois governors, many dignitaries, and thousands of local residents. The Illinois Vietnam Veterans Memorial and Illinois Korean War Memorial, located in the cemetery, are visited by hundreds of thousands of people each year.

Springfield offers the sports fan numerous outlets for cheering their favorite teams, like the Springfield Junior Blues Hockey team and collegiate sports such as the University of Illinois men's Prairie Stars soccer, Lincoln Land Community College baseball, and Springfield College in Illinois' new soccer teams. And of course the city and surrounding area is alive with high school sports competition typified in "March Madness" at the height of basketball season. But the local schools have swimming, golf, baseball, hockey, volleyball, tennis, track and field, and football teams as well. Racing enthusiasts can experience the thrill of automobile and motorcycle racing events such as the Allen Crowe Memorial 100 Race and the Springfield Mile, held at the Illinois State Fairground's famous dirt track. Over a dozen golf courses are located

Henson Robinson Childrens' Zoo at Lake Springfield is home to over 200 animals from across the world, including endangered species. Among its lemurs, penguins, and monkeys, one of the most popular is the resident groundhog, prognosticator of spring's arrival time. Photo by Terry Farmer

A lone jogger glides past an elaborate flower border in a city park. Springfield parks provide recreational outlets for athletes and nature lovers of all ages. Photo by Terry Farmer

The magic of discovery never ends at the Illinois State Museum. Founded to explore the natural history of the state, the museum also features an outstanding decorative arts collection focusing on Illinois, and its young peoples' Discovery Room is filled with games and learning experiences. Photo by Terry Farmer

in the metropolitan area where tens of thousands of rounds are played each year. The LPGA State Farm Classic is staged every Labor Day weekend at The Rail Golf Club in Sherman, Illinois and hosts national champions.

The arts burst upon the scene the first day of the year with First Night Springfield, a festival offering dance, mimes, theater, musicians, and other live performances. But the arts live here year round as well. The city is home to the Muni Opera, Springfield Theatre Guild, Illinois Symphony Orchestra, Springfield Art Association, art galleries, the Springfield Area Arts Council, and much more. The Sangamon Auditorium Concert Series at the University of Illinois at Springfield is known for bringing a diverse range of acts to the city each year. The new venue for the arts is the downtown Springfield Center for the Arts, the former Masonic Temple with auditoriums, audition rooms, and conference areas. It promises to be a true center for city arts.

Museums play an important role in preserving history and Springfield has a splendid variety of museums located throughout the city. Besides the Lincoln attractions, with its historic house museums, Springfield is home to the Illinois State Museum, Springfield Children's Museum, Route 66 museum, and many others. By far the largest in the city, the Illinois State Museum presents the state's natural history as well as art and cultural heritage. Illinois' military past is well documented by the Illinois State Military Museum located at Camp Lincoln, the Grand Army of the Republic Museum, and the Daughters of Union Veterans headquarters. Nostalgic artifacts of the "Mother Road" can be viewed at Bill Shea's Route 66 Museum. The new Lincoln Presidential Library and Museum will have a worldwide presence as it draws visitors from many countries.

Fairs and festivals are held in the Springfield area throughout the year. The granddaddy of all fairs, the Illinois State Fair, opens for a week every August and attracts tens of thousands of visitors who come to eat the traditional fair food fare, take in the exhibits, watch the acts, attend concerts, and view the livestock. But the Illinois State Fairgrounds are busy for the rest of the year. In fact the fairgrounds' buildings are home to a number of national horse and cattle shows that are held every year as well. A new multipurpose arena at the

Fun comes in many packages —in the form of a carousel or waterslide are just two of those. Water parks, playgrounds, and recreation of all sorts offer locals a chance to come out and play. Photos by Terry Farmer

The Illinois State Fair, established in 1852, has evolved from primarily an agricultural exhibition to a summer entertainment venue. Animal barns and exhibits of farm machinery are now joined by big name entertainment; horse, auto, and motorcycle racing; folk dancers, and the carnival midway. Amusement rides are a favorite destination for thrill-seeking fairgoers. The rising August moon casts a warm glow over this scene at dusk. Photo by Terry Farmer

The Illinois State Fair's Ethnic Village brings old world customs and pride to fair visitors. Participants come from all across the state to celebrate the ethnic heritage of Czechs, Poles, African-Americans, Italians, and others. Music plays a big part, too, in evoking a culture, but dance and food are there in abundance as well. In contrast to the lively, crowded festival is a meditative New Salem (opposite) awakening to a blanketing of snow. The little village near Springfield that nurtured a fledgling Abraham Lincoln has been recreated for a new generation of visitors. Photos by Terry Farmer

fairgrounds was added to bring in rodeos and provide another venue for outdoor concerts. The Sangamon County Fair, located in New Berlin, Illinois offers the same atmosphere but on a smaller, county fair scale. Events like the Washington Street Jazz Festival and the Carillon Festival attract crowds of people seeking an evening of music under the stars. Other festivals like the local Ethnic Festival combine food, music, and dancing. For over 40 years, the Old Capital Art Fair has been providing artists a chance to present their works to shoppers looking for a unique piece to adorn their house or body.

Those seeking their kicks on Route 66 can enjoy the new International Route 66 Mother Road Festival "anchored in downtown Springfield with a nostalgic atmosphere complete with cars sporting tailfins and sock hops to oldies music." From operetta to soccer, sports, and arts aficionados will find plenty to do in Springfield. *S*

A gardener's world in Springfield is a happy one of temperate climate, rich soils, and a large variety of natives and exotics that grow lavishly from April through October. Nurseries filled with flourishing selections, public gardens, and a civic garden club are all available to local garden enthusiasts. Photo by Terry Farmer

84 Springfield

(above) **W**ater sports are popular in Springfield. Iron Horse Triathlon participants converge on Lake Springfield annually. The lake opened in the 1930s and is the source for Springfield's water supply. Photo by Terry Farmer

(right) **T**he Nelson Center in Springfield's Lincoln Park is a great place for family swimming fun. The public facility also offers ice skating and Junior Blues hockey. Photo by Terry Farmer

Springfield 87

chapter|eight

8

A SPECIAL SPIRIT

Springfield is a community of neighborhoods. Whether the houses are old, new, or "in-between," kids' summer activities are pretty much the same: playing games, bike riding, hanging out with friends, or the favorite for budding entrepreneurs—opening a lemonade stand. Photo by Terry Farmer

Little League baseball teams are a familiar sight in summertime Springfield. Enthusiastic players and parents crowd the diamonds. But sometimes you're just too young, even for Little League. This little guy waits for his time at the plate. Photo by Terry Farmer

While some factors that contribute to Springfield's quality of life are easily measured —employment statistics, economic growth, and business development—others are less tangible, but their effects create ripples of satisfaction and contentment. An act of kindness by a neighbor or church member or an anonymous donation to a charity all help to make Springfield the livable place it is. From the simple act of one neighbor helping another with painting or mowing the lawn, through church volunteer groups to the large, formally-organized charities like United Way, Springfield is a place of old-fashioned caring and cooperation.

Springfield has many charities and volunteer groups staffed by people who give of their time, talents, and resources to make like better for others. Helping out ranges from caring for abandoned animals to providing food, clothing, and shelter for the homeless. From building a house for a low-income family to housing a family after a fire, the needs are endless.

The city has countless charities, many familiar to all citizens, including Goodwill, Salvation Army, Catholic Charities, Big Brother/Big Sister, and the American Red Cross, Helping Hands, St. John's Breadline, Habitat for Humanity, and Ronald McDonald House. And there are

lesser known, but vital ones like Mini O'Beirne Crisis Nursery, Springfield Community Foundation, Family Service Center, Friend in Deed, and Fifth Street Renaissance, all providing much-needed help and support—financial, emotional, and medical.

In recent years, community service has manifested itself in the form of neighborhood associations which have organized across the city. These associations are, in so many ways, outgrowths of neighbors looking out for one another. Whether it's Enos Park Neighborhood Association residents organizing clean-up days, or West Side Neighborhood members rallying around a quality of life issue, the goal is the same, people helping one another for the benefit of all. There are dozens of neighborhood associations: Harvard Park, Hawthorne Place, Lindsay Place, Mather and Wells, The North End Improvement, Lake Shore Improvement, and Westchester to name only a few. These associations represent every section of town and every type of neighborhood from historic to just-built. But, whether inner-city or suburban, all have one thing in common, they exist on volunteer effort.

A rich and diverse religious community provides opportunities for people of all faiths for worship and uplift. Springfield is home to many religious congregations with over 120 places of worship. Roman Catholicism has a strong presence in the city which serves as the seat for the diocese of central Illinois. The diocese, comprised of 28 counties covers the entire width of central Illinois from Danville on the east to Quincy on the west. Over 100 parishes and missions, including ten in Springfield

itself, are administered by the dioceses. Educational institutions like colleges, high schools, and parochial schools also make up the diocese as do hospitals. Besides the Catholic diocese, Springfield is also the seat for an Episcopal Diocese which was established in 1876. This diocese covers southern Illinois and is comprised of 44 parishes and missions including three in Springfield, Cathedral Church of Saint Paul, Christ Episcopal, and Saint Luke's Episcopal. Most of the Protestant denominations are represented in Springfield including but not limited to Methodists, Baptists, Presbyterians, Lutherans, and Church of Christ. Four synagogues, Temple Israel, Children of the Light Messianic Congregation, Petah Tikvah Messianic Jewish Congregation, and Temple B'rith Sholom, serve members of the Jewish faith.

Before the 20th century the single most important source of social services in a community was usually found in its churches. Church members felt responsible to feed and clothe the poor, help new families settle in the community, and assist families visited by tragedy—illness

Springfield is protected by a corps of dedicated firefighters and police. With a long tradition of community service, both departments have second and third generation members. A new main fire station is supplemented by engine houses like this located around town. Photo by Terry Farmer

The volunteer spirit is a strong value in Springfield. Here a red-coated courtesy guide makes life easier for hospital visitors. Photo by Terry Farmer

or loss of a home, for example. Ministers and priests were typically spiritual and social counselors, listening to and advising on marriage or emotional problems. Despite the network of social service agencies that has grown up in the 20th century, the church is often still where people turn first in time of need.

Service clubs and organizations abound, each filling a special need in the community—the Lions, Optimists, Altrusa, Frontiers International, American Association of University Women, Rotary, Sertoma (literally "Service to Mankind"), League of Women Voters, Jaycees, and Kiwanis being only a very few of the better-known service groups. Fraternal organizations including Odd Fellows, Eastern Star, Elks, Shriners, Masons, and Knights of Columbus perform countless hours of community service every year. Big Brother/Big Sister of Sangamon County and the Boys and Girls Club of Springfield give caring and concerned adults a chance to work with young people and instilling in them the value of giving to others. Traditional groups like Parent Teachers Associations and Woman's Club have been joined in recent years by groups like The Susan B. Anthony/Harriett Tubman Women's Self Help Center and study circles designed to promote racial harmony—both reflective of changing social attitudes about serving community needs.

But a rich strata of volunteerism exists in less-noticed community work too. In the medical field alone the hospitals have volunteer coordinators to organize the large number of people who help with everything from greeting visitors to running hospital gift shops. Springfield doctors and other healthcare workers regularly travel to other countries on medical missionary work. Here in Springfield the medical community regularly provides emergency care or operations to those in need from other places—from Tijuana to Mozambique, children and adults have been brought to Springfield for corrective surgery, free of charge to they and their families. Attorneys provide free or reduced cost legal service individually or with the Land of Lincoln Legal Assistance Foundation. Retired executives mentor others through the Senior Corps of Retired Executives. Others help with tax preparation assistance to the public at no cost. The more vulnerable in the community are helped by volunteers at Sojourn Center for domestic violence, Meals on Wheels for the elderly or homebound, PORA for

Pride in country and a willingness to serve in time of war and peace have characterized generations of Springfieldians. Honoring local veterans has been a significant concern for many as seen in our monuments to those who served in Vietnam, Korea, and the Second World War. This brief exchange among family members captures all the pride of parents and a son. Photo by Terry Farmer

Winter brings its magic to Illinois' capital city when windows and trees glow with holiday lights. The upscale Gables shopping complex takes an especially festive holiday air, chasing away some of the chill of winter. Photo by Terry Farmer

recovering prostitutes, and Washington Street Mission, all of which depend heavily on volunteers.

On the most personal level lives are changed by the people who give time to coach kids' baseball, soccer, or swimming teams, or who help with Make A Wish foundation's work of granting a secret wish to terminally ill children and their families. State Farm Rail Classic golf tournament is just one of the larger local charity events, but typical of the hundreds of fund-raisers, large and small, put together by caring local people every year. These benefit everything from local organizations to a families facing medical or other emergencies.

From helping an adult learn to read for the first time to building a Habitat for Humanity house, Springfield is a place rich in community spirit. *S*

An interpreter at Lincoln's New Salem Historic Site sweeps her front step. Volunteers and a small staff maintain the village for thousands of visitors each month showing them daily life—cooking, gardening, and everyday chores—in a pioneer village. Photo by Terry Farmer

"Our employees have a passion for the construction process. They come to our firm with varying degrees of expertise, and these dedicated individuals use their daily experiences to improve their knowledge and skills. An entrepreneurial spirit pervades the company and a synergy among Siciliano employees assures continued expansion of operations and an ever-increasing reputation for the highest quality, detail, and craftsmanship in every project, large or small. Without the dedication, commitment, and care of its talented employees, Siciliano would never have become a leading presence in central Illinois construction."

Richard E. Lawrence
President
Siciliano, Inc.

(above) **B**ackyard cooking, a staple of summer living, is a favorite local pastime. A Springfield family here shares time together making the necessity of food preparation an enjoyable ritual. "A great place to raise a family" is what natives and newcomers alike say about the town. Photo by Terry Farmer

(right) **S**pringfield loves a parade and one of its favorites is the annual St. Patrick's procession full of bands, floats, candy-tossers, and assorted leprechauns. Two escaped leprechauns take seriously the wearin' of the green. In winter (opposite) city streets are festively garlanded. Historic buildings line downtown streets. Photo by Terry Farmer

94 | Springfield

Springfield is a town of churches, synagogues, and cathedrals, representing every denomination. The quiet grandeur of the Cathedral of the Immaculate Conception is an impressive, awe-inspiring place. Patterned after Roman buildings, the cathedral is the centerpiece of a complex housing the Roman Catholic diocese. Carloads of marble and stone were used in its construction and local officials, dignitaries, and thousands of citizens turned out at its opening in 1928. Photo by Terry Farmer

Photo by Terry Farmer

Part Two

Springfield **101**

chapter | **nine**

9

HIGH TECHNOLOGY, NETWORKS & UTILITIES

Insight Communications, 102-103
Cingular Wireless, 104-105
CIBER, 106
Springfield Mass Transit District, 107
Levi, Ray & Shoup, Inc., 108
Yevich, Lawson and Associates, Inc., 109
CILCO, 110

Photo by Terry Farmer

Insight Communications

Insight employees are committed to top-notch customer service as a key priority.

Customers of Insight Communications have come to expect a lot more than basic cable service from this provider. One of the nation's largest cable operators, Insight offers its million-plus customers a variety of state-of-the-art entertainment, educational, and information services in each of the many communities it serves. Headquartered in New York City, Insight has many operations in Illinois—where it is the second-largest cable operator in the state—as well as in Indiana, Kentucky, Ohio, and Georgia. Insight took over the Springfield area's cable operations from the previous operator in January 2001.

The company's primary business is the distribution of information and entertainment programming. Its customers enjoy many channels of news, sports, movies, comedy, drama, and educational programming with the simplicity and reliability of cable's broadband, fiber-optic networks. Insight is also leading the cable industry in developing and providing the services that are becoming part of everyone's future—high-speed Internet access, interactive digital cable, and telephony service.

The infrastructure of Insight's cable system lets customers select from a large menu of services that will be continuously updated and advanced as improved technology becomes available. By implementing this cutting-edge, "future proof" system, Insight is protecting its customers from hardware obsolescence; this enables the company to deploy new technologies more easily and uniformly with all of the latest advancements in entertainment and communication services. Furthermore, Insight's technology means that customers do not need a satellite dish or antenna for clear reception of local channels.

Insight offers customers a diverse array of channels with a variety of entertainment and information options. Basic Cable Service provides clear reception of local broadcast and cable channels and connects customers to additional services. Classic Cable Service offers the most popular cable networks available today, with a broad range of programming that provides something for every member of the family. Numerous premium movie channels and pay-per-view options are also available.

Insight's Springfield system is currently in the process of an $11 million upgrade that will increase bandwidth capacity to 860 megahertz, and should be completed by mid-year 2002. The result will be a two-way, fiber optic system that delivers the highly innovative Insight Digital service, which is on the forefront of interactive television. Insight Digital provides a clearer digital picture with fewer disruptions and doubles the channel capacity of the former channel line-up, both analog and digital. In addition, Insight Digital will introduce two revolutionary products to Springfield—LocalSource and On Demand TV. LocalSource is an interactive community information and entertainment guide created exclusively for Springfield-area customers; it can be used to access local weather, sports, cinema listings, restaurant menus, school activities, and much more. On Demand TV allows customers to browse through hundreds of movie titles and begin viewing a selection at any time, all with the full VCR functionality to rewind, fast-forward, and pause on the cable set-top box. These leading-edge services are available only to a handful of communities nationwide.

The system upgrade also gives Insight customers the opportunity to enjoy high-speed access to the Internet through the same cable lines that provide their television service. This service gives customers a range of high-speed data services at speeds up to one hundred times faster than normal dial-up phone lines—which means no more long waits for large digital files to download.

Insight has also joined forces with AT&T to provide local telephony services in some markets to Insight customers, and is expected to launch in Springfield in 2003. This service will provide a competitive alternative in the local phone arena. Customers who choose this option will receive all of their cable television, Internet, and telephone services on the same cable line, resulting in the convenience of one-stop shopping and discounts for customers who choose multiple services. Representative of the very latest in integrated technology, this "bundled" approach underscores Insight's commitment to staying on the forefront of the very latest in technological innovations.

Yet all of this technology does not mean very much if customers do not quickly and courteously receive customer and technical support when they need it. Therefore, Insight makes customer service its highest priority. As friends and neighbors within Springfield-area communities, Insight's customer service representatives,

Insight's current multimillion dollar rebuild of Springfield's cable system will provide the most leading-edge services in the industry.

installers, and technicians aim to deliver unparalleled service. They are Insight's goodwill ambassadors, offering front-line support to help customers choose programming packages, become educated on new product offerings, and help them solve technical problems, often over the phone.

Among its customer service commitments, Insight joins the cable industry in its On-Time Guarantee initiative, which credits customer accounts if installers fail to arrive on time for a scheduled installation or service appointment. Insight also makes every effort to accommodate customer schedules for service and repair appointments whenever possible and is always committed to improving customer service in additional ways. In fact, in a recent customer service survey, Insight scored well above the cable industry's average on this topic, an achievement for which the company's employees have consistently strived.

Further accolades were awarded to the company when, for its many recent accomplishments, Insight was named "2001 Cable Operator of the Year" by *Cablevision Magazine*.

Insight Communications is an active member of the Springfield-area community. The company offers the use of its channels for local programs that provide heightened awareness and information about community events, issues, and activities. Through an industry-wide initiative called "Cable in the Classroom," Insight also provides free cable service to every elementary, junior, and senior high school in the communities it serves, allowing teachers to create new curricula and innovative learning environments by accessing cable programming. Insight's "In the Know" program takes the commitment to education a step further by providing a free cable modem and monthly service in all eligible schools, as well as by partnering with cable networks to provide robust content and technology to enhance the classroom experience. In addition, Insight employees regularly participate in community programs such as CrimeStoppers, Fleet Watch, and Chamber of Commerce activities.

As Insight continues to grow, it continues to uphold the same values upon which its initial success was based. The company makes significant investments in its people, its operations, and its future to realize its vision: becoming a multifaceted communications business driven by quality customer service.

Cingular Wireless

Cingular's state-of-the-art call center—Springfield's West Side, established 2000. Photo by Terry Farmer

Through aggressive growth Cingular Wireless has become the second largest wireless company in the United States, serving more than 21 million customers in 38 states. In Springfield, this growth has made Cingular a premier employer. From humble beginnings in the late 1980s, Cingular now employs nearly 800 people in the Springfield area and according to *The State Journal-Register* newspaper "is poised to become one of Springfield's largest private employers."

Locally, Cingular's origins began in 1988 with the founding of Crowley Cellular, doing business as Cellular One. The rapidly growing company flourished and in 1991 SBC Communications, Southwestern Bell Mobile Systems, acquired Crowley Cellular, Cellular One. Cingular Wireless was formed in 2001 when the domestic wireless divisions of SBC and Bell South were merged in a joint venture to create Cingular. In January 2001 a 100,000-square-foot Call Center was completed on the city's far west side. The company has since influenced the direction of wireless communication through their technical innovations and creative marketing.

The Cingular Wireless name emphasizes the importance of the individual or "cingular" customer to a company that is dedicated to self-expression and customer-friendly service. The company is determined to promote the individual to a new level and to create a personal relationship with each of its customers. To enhance the ability to communicate, Cingular offers an exciting variety of products including digital wireless, wireless data including text messaging, and Internet services.

Cingular has custom-designed calling plans to meet consumers' needs. Cingular's call plans allow customers to travel anywhere in the United States and pay low rates based on the Plan chosen. Cingular has local, region, and nation plans—they fit every customers need!!

Cingular also offers data based means of communicating through interactive messaging and Internet connection. Interactive messaging features mobile to mobile messaging for sending short text messages between Cingular digital phones, e-mail messages and access to news, stock quotes, sports scores, and other information.

Facing challenges of attracting new customers, increased competition, and maintaining current customer satisfaction, Cingular strives to serve all consumer levels from corporate to small business to the man on the street. Cingular focuses on the two main categories of customers: corporate and retail. The corporate team works with businesses to design and plan solutions to fill their needs. There are three types of retail outlets located throughout the city—Authorized Agents, Company-Owned Stores, and Retail Distributors. These outlets sell and service the wireless products offered by Cingular and sometimes other products such as car stereos, TV, or satellite networks.

The Springfield Call Center is responsible for responding to questions and concerns

Cingular Wireless employees keep them number one. Photo by Terry Farmer

The design of the Cingular Wireless Retail location emphasizes fun and self expression through interactive displays, bold advertising, and knowledgable sales staff. Photo by Terry Farmer

regarding billing, phone usage, and technical questions. The call center is currently equipped to handle over 20,000 calls per day. Finding enough qualified employees to man the 700 jobs at the center was viewed by some as being a problem in the Springfield market because of the area's low unemployment rates. Company Officials were not concerned because Springfield has proven to have a good quality work force and a good quality of life.

Cingular's innovations have set the standard for wireless communication in Central Illinois. Cingular was the first wireless company to have an all-digital network serving a six state region—Illinois, Wisconsin, Michigan, Indiana, Kentucky, and Ohio. The local Cingular service region, including Springfield, encompasses the communities of Bloomington to the north, Champaign on the east, Quincy on the west, and Salem on the south. Its state-of-the-art network is based on an all-digital global system for mobile communications (GSM) technology for mobile phone users GSM is the fastest growing wireless communications technology in the world today.

Cingular is committed, not only to providing the highest quality wireless service, but also to enriching their communities through cultural and charitable sponsorship.

Cingular Wireless's community commitment is as important as customer service. Corporate direction leads Cingular to help communities express and enhance their unique characteristics thru volunteer service and donation programs. Cingular's staff seek local solutions to community needs. Cingular employees' volunteer spirit is a key element in community relations. The Springfield Cingular organization has been a major sponsor of the Ironhorse Triathlon and the LPGA State Farm Classic golf tournament. Cingular is involved with the local Easter Seals campaign, Special Olympics program, United Way, and Ronald McDonald House.

From the pioneering days of cellular telephone development to today's virtual worldwide access, Cingular consistently strives to provide the best product. The company's vision is to expand by offering customers advanced technologies in simple, cost effective terms. Cingular cares about the individual and how they can meet their ever changing needs. Cingular listens when they ask, "What do you have to say?"

CIBER

The networking consulting practice provides PC and network Support.

Successful businesses and organizations embrace innovation and change and look to CIBER (www.ciber.com), a computer-consulting corporation providing service offerings and information technology solutions that reflect their extensive industry knowledge and experience. CIBER's services span all components of today's technology solutions: Strategy and Enterprise Integration, Internet Services, Business Intelligence, Network Integration/Security, Wireless, and Outsourcing. Founded in 1974, CIBER (NYSE: CBR) has 5,000 employees in 60 cities nationwide and is headquartered in Englewood, Colorado.

The CIBER Springfield office was opened when Ed Burns (now Senior Vice President but then a technical consultant) was sent to Springfield on assignment with five or six others in the 1970s. Burns recognized the possibilities for business growth and, in 1982, established a Cutler/Williams office (then the company's name) in Springfield. When Joe Marchizza, Regional Vice President for the Springfield office, joined the company as a technical consultant in 1987, there were about 20 employees. Today the Springfield office employs over 150 persons. The story of CIBER employees rising to management levels is a common one in Springfield. For a fast-paced industry, there is a surprisingly low turnover in CIBER staff. This has created a family business atmosphere that benefits both clients and employees. Clients are able to build a business relationship of trust and confidence with people they have come to know, yet who also have the resources of a large, nationwide corporation.

CIBER's employees feel they are a part of the CIBER family, not an unknown commodity, and many have become active members of the Springfield community. The Springfield CIBER office is actively involved in the community through sponsorship of events and organizations such as Big Brothers/Big Sisters, the Festival of Trees, American Heart Association, American Cancer Society, the Mini O'Beirne Crisis Nursery, Illinois Central Blues Club, and the State Farm Rail Classic, a charitable golf fundraiser.

The Springfield office primarily provides information technology solutions to local, state, and federal agencies and three large sectors of private industry—insurance, manufacturing, and telecommunications. The key areas of technology in which CIBER's consultants support their clients include network management, project management, client/server and mainframe applications development, as well as e-commerce and data warehousing solutions. CIBER consultants work with a number of different product platforms while the company continues to build its alliances with today's technology leaders to provide unmatched technology prowess. For example, CIBER's Springfield office is a Microsoft Certified Solution Provider, with a number of technical consultants providing service to clients as Microsoft certified product specialists, system engineers, and software developers.

Employees spend approximately 90 to 95 percent of their time on-site assisting clients and customers. In some instances, for example, employees work with a client daily providing network or project management. At other times, consultants are needed for short-term support or troubleshooting capabilities. In addition, CIBER works not only to provide software solutions but also with clients needing assistance with hardware decisions. Consultants perform the analysis, make recommendations, and can help procure the equipment.

With more than 25 years in the information technology business and an office in Springfield for over 20 years, CIBER's leading-edge expertise, experience, and insight into the IT industry offers customers a personalized and efficient service with high-value results. Such quality service has enabled the company to maintain success and provide stability to its employees and clients in a competitive and ever-changing industry.

Consultants analyze information systems issues and develop customized solutions for them.

Springfield Mass Transit District

The Springfield Mass Transit District serves Springfield in dozens of ways. Whether providing rides to its customers, contributing to the economic growth of the city, or running environmentally efficient vehicles, the Springfield Mass Transit District (SMTD) strives to be a good neighbor and beneficial partner to the community. Historically Springfield has had public transportation systems since the 1860s. However, with the creation of a tax-funded district established by referendum vote in February, 1968, SMTD began its service to Capitol, Springfield and Woodside townships in July of that year. People from all ages and economic groups are served, including those who are unable to use the fixed-route buses. Access Springfield provides curb-to-curb service for those who qualify under the Americans with Disabilities Act. With approval of an application, they can call Access Springfield to schedule a ride. Discounted fares are offered through passes on the fixed-route system and the elderly and persons with disabilities and appropriate ID ride anytime at a discounted rate.

The SMTD fleet includes 49 buses, 90 percent of which are wheelchair-lift equipped. Eighteen of the buses are fueled by energy-efficient and environmentally-friendly compressed natural gas. The SMTD was one of the first transit systems in Illinois to convert to alternatively fueled vehicles and one of very few to select compressed natural gas. Daily operating hours for SMTD and Access Springfield run from 6:00 a.m. to 6:00 p.m. Monday through Saturday. During the Illinois State Fair, SMTD Shuttle buses run from the downtown area to the main gate of the fairgrounds. Both SMTD and Access Springfield vehicles operate late enough for fairgoers to enjoy the grandstand shows and have a ride home.

In 1999, the SMTD was designated as the first Regional Maintenance Center in Illinois by the Illinois Department of Transportation (IDOT). The maintenance staff at SMTD possess the special knowledge and expertise to repair vehicles that have additional equipment and safety systems. The vehicles maintained in this program have been purchased by IDOT for use by rural transit providers and social service agencies throughout the State.

The SMTD also has been a leader in the transit industry in the use of video surveillance cameras on its vehicles. It was among the first in the country to install cameras on its entire fleet. Although crime has been virtually non-existent on the buses, the cameras provide an added element of security for the passengers. The cameras deter graffiti, vandalism, and fraudulent claims as well. The cameras also have been beneficial as a teaching tool for drivers and have assisted with maintenance issues.

The SMTD will continue in its efforts to improve the system, to grow with the city, and to provide the best possible service to the community.

Whether providing rides to its customers, contributing to the economic growth of the city, or running environmentally efficient vehicles, SMTD strives to be a good neighbor and beneficial partner to the community. Photo by Terry Farmer

The SMTD fleet includes 49 buses, 90 percent of which are wheelchair-lift equipped. Photo by Terry Farmer

Levi, Ray & Shoup, Inc.

LRS corporate headquarters fills an office complex on West Monroe Street.

Levi, Ray & Shoup, Inc., one of the Springfield area's most phenomenal success stories, has a history of technological excellence and innovation. Founded by three friends in 1979, LRS has grown to become a global provider of innovative information technology solutions with more than 550 employees. From corporate headquarters in Springfield, LRS operates six offices in the United States and five more around the globe: Madrid, Spain; Frankfort and Munich, Germany; Cheltenham, England; and Sydney, Australia. A network of 13 international distributors also markets LRS software, which is used by a majority of Fortune 500 firms and in more than 30 countries around the world. The company is ranked by *Software Magazine* as one of the top 200 software companies in the world.

When they founded LRS in 1979, partners Dick Levi, Roger Ray, and Bob Shoup specialized in providing consulting services to a variety of local companies and state agencies. Ray and Shoup eventually sold their share to Dick Levi. As the company matured, it developed products and services in specific information technology areas.

• In 1981 LRS developed the first software that enabled MVS mainframe systems to distribute output to printers outside the data center. Today LRS leads the industry in Enterprise Output Management products, and its core product, VTAM Printer Support (VPS®), runs on more than 5,000 mainframes worldwide.

• LRS IT Solutions continues the LRS consulting tradition, providing custom application development, hardware, networking, and software consulting services. An IBM Premier Business Partner, LRS IT Solutions operates one of only 60 IBM TotalStorage Solution Centers in the US and sells a variety of computer hardware. Microsoft Gold Certified Partner status also recognizes our consulting expertise.

• LRS PensionGold software helps pension plan administrators automate data tracking and administrative tasks to increase productivity and member satisfaction.

• LRS Education Services, certified by Microsoft and Novell, provides networking, network management, and productivity software training to organizations and individuals.

• LRSSports Software Systems offers products focusing on the full range of needs of athletic programs at the high school, collegiate, and professional levels.

• LRS Web Services offers clients complete Web site services from creative design through site layout, page building, and custom business applications.

• Information Services provides data processing services for numerous clients.

Today LRS fills an impressive office complex on West Monroe. But the company's commitment to the community is more than buildings; it is also financial support and participation in civic projects, charities, and non-profit groups. LRS sponsors local NHRA funny car driver Tim Wilkerson and is a major sponsor of the annual LPGA State Farm Classic golf tournament.

An international firm dedicated to advancing technology, LRS serves its clients and our community with distinction.

Employees and visitors enjoy the patio outside the LRS cafeteria.

Yevich, Lawson and Associates, Inc.

YLA Headquarters are located at 340 West Miller Street.

Yevich, Lawson and Associates, Inc. was formed in 1999 with the merger of the Springfield firm of Lawson and Associates, Inc. and RYC, Inc. of Austin, Texas. Company principals Richard Yevich, Susan Lawson (President), and Alexander Lawson have over a half-century of combined database analysis, design, and development experience. Richard and Susan are internationally recognized consultants and educators known for their expertise in enterprise information systems. They are members of the IBM DB2 Gold Consultant's program and have been honored on many occasions as Best Speakers at events worldwide. They specialize in e-commerce, data warehousing, distributed relational systems across multiple platforms, and in establishing proper design to achieve the highest possible system performance and availability. Richard and Susan have co-authored three books: *DB2 Answers!*, *DB2 High Performance Design and Tuning*, and *DB2 Universal Database for OS/390 Certification Guide for V. 7*.

Alex Lawson is an expert in many applications including Unix, Microsoft, and Macromedia products with a strong background in product development, database design, and Web applications. He has developed systems for both commercial enterprises and government agencies, and performed as a system administrator on numerous Unix/Oracle systems.

Yevich, Lawson and Associates offers consulting services in all areas of database design, large data warehouses, SQL coding, application design, performance audits and reviews, web development, and e-commerce. YL&A recruits and screens its technology professionals in a rigorous and selective process that will ensure that every client receives the best available professional services.

YL&A also provides the best in DB2 education. All instructors are available internationally. Courses can be tailored to meet the specific needs of any organization, including hands-on workshops and labs where applicable. Course categories range from concept and design to performance and administration, data sharing, and warehousing.

Yevich, Lawson and Associates, Inc. continues to expand as demand for database services and e-commerce increase. Technology and Web-based solutions are crucial to any business seeking to remain vital and competitive in the 21st century.

YLA corporate suite, 340 West Miller Street.

CILCO

CILCO has been serving the public utility needs of Springfield since 1854 when the Springfield Gas and Light Company, a private enterprise, was formed. That company was taken over in 1903 by a utility that became Illinois Power Company and reorganized as Central Illinois Light Company (CILCO) in 1933. Today CILCO is known in Central Illinois as *the* supplier of electricity and natural gas to businesses and homes, serving over 250,000 electric and gas customers. Recognizing that competition in the electric and natural gas business was inevitable; CILCO's responsible leadership has taken a pro-consumer approach in the world of deregulation. A concerted effort in planning and maintenance cost control put CILCO in an enviable competitive position resulting in low rates and high customer satisfaction.

But CILCO's success in delivering natural gas and electricity is only the beginning of its community involvement. The company is a community service leader in the fields of education, sports, family entertainment, and economic development. Since 1987, CILCO has participated in the Springfield Public School's Partnership in Education Program in which the company "adopted" Matheny Elementary School. Under this program, CILCO employees tutor Matheny students. CILCO also donated money for a Multi-Cultural Center for use by all district teachers as well as sponsoring scholarships for Matheny students attending summer enrichment programs at Lincoln Land Community College. Other educational programs supported by CILCO include those at the Springfield Urban League and Boys and Girls Club.

CILCO is a prime sponsor of local sporting activities including the University of Illinois at Springfield's soccer program and the Junior Blues Hockey team and Springfield Capitols baseball team. The putting challenge event at the State Farm Rail Classic golf tournament is also underwritten by a CILCO grant.

Public entertainment for area residents receives a boost through CILCO's underwriting of the Summer Serenade Series of free concerts in downtown Springfield, Illinois Symphony Orchestra programs and Sangamon Auditorium performances. CILCO also sponsors one of the theme areas at the Illinois State Fair each year.

In addition to supporting membership in the Greater Springfield Chamber of Commerce, CILCO is one of two corporate sponsors of the Economic Development Council. Company employees are encouraged to become involved in community service, and have charitable donations matched by CILCO, thus leveraging their giving.

Through almost 150 years of serving Springfield, CILCO has defined what it means to be a successful leading energy provider in the United States.

CILCO's commitment to the community includes employee volunteer tutoring each week. Matheny Elementary School is the company's "adopted" school since 1987. Photo by Terry Farmer

American English was one of the bands playing in the Summer Serenades, a 2001 company-sponsored free summer concert. Photo courtesy of The State Journal-Register.

Photo by Terry Farmer

Springfield 113

chapter ten

10

MANUFACTURING & DISTRIBUTION

Brandt Consolidated, Inc., 114-115
Nudo Products, Inc., 116-117
Solomon Colors, 118
Mel-O-Cream Donuts International, 119
Phoenix International, 120

Photo by Terry Farmer

Brandt Consolidated, Inc.

The ClawEl Specialty Products Division develops new products for high value crop applications.

Pioneer farmers of the early 1800s, discovering huge crop yields, knew they had a gold mine in the soils of central Illinois. Some of these farmers made their planting and harvesting decisions based on phases of the moon or the position of a particular planet in the nighttime sky. But, it is unlikely that they ever dreamed of a man-made satellite orbiting the earth aiding them in making crop decisions. Today, Brandt Consolidated is assisting farmers with this space-age technology and more. Their products, services, and advice yield successful crops not only in central Illinois but all over the world.

As with the pioneer farmer, Glen Brandt began small having just one truck for hauling and spraying liquid fertilizer. Brandt and his sister Evelyn Brandt Thomas established Brandt Fertilizer in 1953 near New Berlin, west of Springfield. In 1957 they moved into an office in Pleasant Plains and, in 1967 added Brandt Chemical to the business. Pleasant Plains is still the home of what is today, Brandt Consolidated, made up of three divisions—retail, dealer support, and ClawEl with Glen Brandt's son, Rick, as President/CEO of this progressive company.

The ClawEl Division that manufactures and packages micronutrients and adjuvants, has established a worldwide market. Trace elements (including boron, zinc, manganese, copper) make up micronutrients that enhance plants to be all they can be. A micronutrient can enrich nutritional value, for example, or boost a physical characteristic, like firmer skin on a tomato. Providing quality, not just quantity, is Brandt's goal for their customers. These enhancing products are shipped all around the world. Citrus growers, nurseries raising ornamentals, vegetable growers from the United States, Mexico, South America, Europe, and the Middle East all take advantage of these micronutrient products. The use of adjuvants improves the performance of pesticides. These Brandt products help growers and their consumers benefit directly from improved crops. Specialized fertilizers and turf nutrients are also part of the ClawEl Division.

Brandt Consolidated's retail business is award winning. Ten central Illinois locations—Pleasant Plains, New Berlin, Ashland, Waverly, Curran, Auburn, Franklin, Oakford, Greenview, and Raymond-provide a one-stop-shopping approach for customers whether its seed for planting, feed for livestock, herbicides for weed control, or propane for farm and home. Certified Crop Advisors work directly with farmers in accessing needs based on the most recent information and technology available. Fully trained employees, knowledgeable of restrictions and regulatory requirements, offer custom applications of fertilizers and chemicals.

The Certified Crop Advisors use their knowledge and expertise of the latest edge of agriculture.

The High Q Decision Support system is Brandt's vision of 21st century agriculture. Already, numerous farmers in the central Illinois area are on board with this site-specific method of farming. Brandt supplies a laptop computer and the program software for growers to collect site-specific data such as tillage practices, planting date, seed selection, and nitrogen rates. Using a GPS (global positioning system) antenna mounted on the farmer's combine, yield information is gathered at harvest time. A powerful computer then adds necessary soil, climate, and community information. After analysis the farmer can then make management decisions for crop variety, nutrient and crop protection needs for specific fields or even specific areas within fields based on the statistical data. A record is kept of the information for comparison and adjustments in future years. Brandt's own professionals train growers in the High Q system and are there with technical support and assistance as needed.

Its greatest resource is its people.

For the farmer with a computer and an Internet server, the Brandt Web site offers up-to-date-weather, local news, cash market bids for the local area, and other marketing information. On-line ordering with personal account status is in the planning stage and will be available on the Web site 24 hours a day. Grid soil sampling, crop scouting, tissue sampling, and a CystStopper Program are a few of the other services offered.

Brandt's high level of customer service in the field, site-specific technology, technical support, and Internet services has won them the prestigious Ag Retailer of the Year Award for 2000. President/CEO Rick Brandt gives credit to the exceptional dedication and qualification of the staff. Over 100 employees, from secretarial help to warehouse workers to custom applicators, receive on-going skill development training. This staff gives credibility to the company's slogan, "Professional Agriculture." Rick Brandt's pride in his employees is evident.

Brandt's Dealer Support Division offers independent retailers the same fertilizer products, decision support system, and technical support given to its own retail customers. Fertilizer terminals are open 24 hours a day. Partnering with Brandt allows independents to have a wider range of products, better assist their customers with management, and the technical knowledge of today's agriculture business and still compete with large corporate dealers.

From one truck for spraying liquid fertilizer in 1953 to computer and satellite technology, Brandt has pioneered and grown into a worldwide provider and partner in professional agriculture.

The Retail Division maintains 10 plants in Sangamon and surrounding counties to service the needs of the farmers.

Nudo Products, Inc.

Since the 1990s a new product or building space has been added almost every year at Nudo Products.

Imagine an ice skating surface that requires no water, no refrigeration, no dehumidification, little surface maintenance, that installs at a lower cost than real ice and retains the best characteristics of actual ice for skating. Such a product is made in Springfield by Nudo Products, Inc. It is called Nu-Ice, a synthetic product with a very slick, durable surface.

Receptive and inventive are two words that come to mind in describing the owners of Nudo Products: receptive to new ideas and opportunities that fall within their manufacturing, marketing, and distribution capabilities and inventive in that new products trigger ideas for others, some of which they patent. Nu-Ice is only the most obvious example of Nudo's innovative thinking.

It all began in August of 1954, when Sam Nudo, Sr. joined his brother in establishing Economy Awning and Tile Company, a retail shop selling awnings, floor tile, siding, and windows. In 1962 Sam bought out his brother and kept hold of a dream to one day sell his own products rather than someone else's. The opportunity arrived when Armbruster Manufacturing in Springfield decided to stop fabricating fiberglass awnings. Sam investigated, acquired the equipment, and set about adding his own ideas to the designs. Economy Awning became a wholesaler and the largest fiberglass awning-manufacturing dealer in Illinois. Sam and his wife, Wanda raised five sons, each of whom has been involved with Nudo Products. Wanda, herself, took an active place, serving as president of the firm. Today, three of the boys, Sam Jr., Tim, and Pat are the main partners in the business, while Sam, Sr. calls himself one of their employees.

The bulkiness of fiberglass awnings and consequent shipping costs limited their market area, so in the late 1970s, when the company was approached about manufacturing fiberglass panels for the dairy, farm, and food processing industry, they seized the opportunity. Nudo Products hasn't been the same since. Sam Nudo, Sr. gives a lot of credit for the expansions to his sons, who have followed their father's lead in being open to new prospects. While fiberglass awnings and the wind deflectors for the recreational vehicle industry (for which Sam Sr. has a patent) are still made, they are less than one percent of the hundreds of products manufactured, marketed, and distributed nationally and internationally today.

Nudo manufacturing process for laminating fiberglass to plywood panels opened the doors to numerous other paneling systems using aluminum, vinyl, and plastic. These laminates are bonded to foam cores, waferboard, OSB, particleboard, and various other substrates. They can be single or double sided, in finishes that are smooth or textured with choices of patterns and colors. Used in floors, ceilings, walls, partitions, signs, and countertops, these products are odor, chemical, stain, scratch, shatter, and moisture resistant. They clean with steam, detergent and water, or high pressure sprayers and do not trap dirt or food particles. They are ideal for use in restaurants,

Left to right: Matt Campbell, Eric McMillan, Chris Collins, George Drobnack, Pat Nudo, John Bednarko, and Mark Simpson.

food processing plants, dog kennels, modular buildings, restrooms, schools, car washes, hospitals—the number of applications is immense—anywhere a durable, sanitary, easily maintained construction material is needed. Distributors, architects, and contractors readily recognize the registered and trademarked names such as Fiber-Lite®, Nu-Poly®, Nu-Alum®, and FiberCorr®. Thousands of various panels are produced each day.

Through imaginative thinking, the laminating process led naturally to the manufacture of plastic profile pieces—moldings, corners, caps, and other pieces that join and finish panels. Special equipment that turns vinyl or plastic pellets into a liquid forced continuously through a die, manufactures the desired shape profile extrusions, and length. Next came an injection molding system that forces various resins into a mold to make rivets, screws, and other fasteners that will not rust, rot, peel, or corrode and are used to attach paneling to wood, brick, stone, concrete, or other substrates. One of the newer processes for Nudo Products is sheet extrusion. This works much as the profile extrusion except that a continuous flow of plastic or vinyl material produces sheets up to 60 inches wide, in various thicknesses, into rolls weighing up to 1000 pounds. With this process Nudo has become its own best customer through vertical integration. No longer do they buy the plastic and vinyl sheets they laminate. They also market their plastic sheets to various case manufacturers who produce things such as band instrument and computer cases.

With their own machining capabilities at Nudo, laminated panels can be tongue and grooved or cut to shapes and routed for counter and table tops. New product lines keep coming. A new edge treatment process applies a durable plastic coating to routed edges. New heat laminating equipment reduces curing time and adds flexibility in production of products using foam cores over the original cold press laminating systems. And then there are Nu-Ice, a product improved over other earlier synthetic ice and Nudo's beautiful exotic solid wood and engineered wood flooring and garden teak tiles. The extensive distribution network established at Nudo enhances new product capabilities.

Since the 1990s a new product or building space has been added almost every year at Nudo Products.

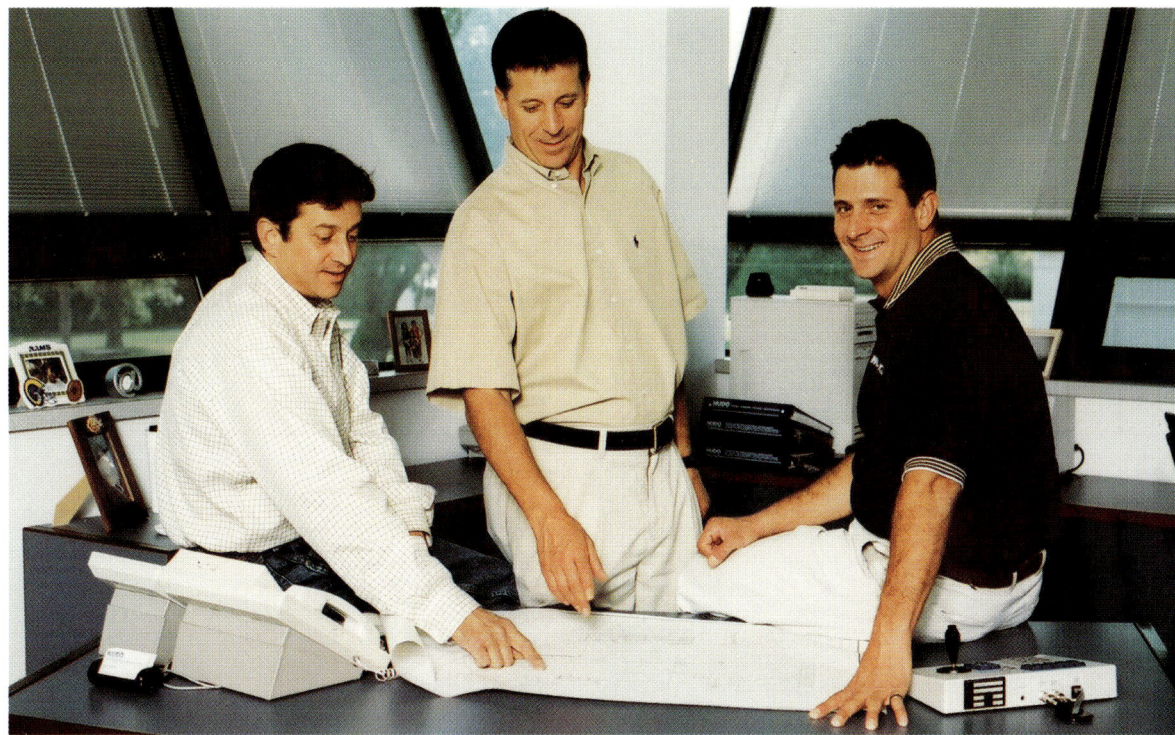

The three owners of Nudo Products, Inc., left to right: Tim Nudo, Sam Nudo, Jr., and Pat Nudo.

The manufacturer now has over 150 employees. The laminating, profile, and sheet extrusion and injection molding processes combined with their machining and distribution systems allows for extensive flexibility in product production. While new lines keep the company vibrant, its focus is kept on good customer service, competitive prices, and quality. Service, quality, and unique products are what has built Nudo Products Inc.'s reputation as a manufacturer and wholesaler and keeps it growing.

The founder of Nudo Products, Inc., Sam Nudo, Sr. and his son Pat Nudo.

Solomon Colors

Richard Solomon, Vice President (left) and Robert Solomon, President (right) proudly display a pallet of 25lb ready mix color bags, 4,000lb ColorFlo™ liquid tote, and a pallet of concentrated motor color cases.

From coast to coast, color in concrete and masonry is much in demand by architects and their clients. Contractors and manufacturers look to Solomon Colors for the pigments that turn mortar, pavers, roof tile, stucco, grout, concrete brick, and precast and poured-in-place concrete products, into aesthetically pleasing architectural features. This Springfield based company is the largest U.S.-owned producer of iron oxide pigments.

In 1927 when Robert Christopher Solomon, was the operator of the Panther Creek Coal Mine Co. he investigated the possibility of utilizing the black, carboniferous slate, that laid above the coal seam, as a color by-product from the mining operations. Thus began the grinding and pulverizing business, Solomon Grinding Company. He used the slate from the mines for the coloring he sold to the mortar and cement industry and combined rail shipments of red iron ore from Michigan and yellow ochres from Georgia to grind and blend for colors as well as for the foundry and trace mineral industries.

As the business climate changed, iron oxide pigments became Solomon's main product. In the 1970s the company's name changed to Solomon Grind-Chem Services to better represent its use of synthetic iron oxides in addition to grinding natural oxides. Today, Solomon Colors continues the family tradition started by Robert C. Solomon with his son and grandson involved in the business.

Based on combinations of just three iron oxide colors —yellow, red, and black—Solomon Colors' catalog lists over 500 standard pigment shades. Additionally, more than twice that number have been custom blended for architects and contractors seeking to match existing materials or wanting a specialized color. The stable, colorfast pigments are sold in dry form or liquid to the concrete, masonry, and ready-mix industries.

The innovation of Solomon Colors' ColorSelect™ Liquid Dispensing System is changing the concrete product production industry by allowing ready-mix, precast, concrete block, and paver producers to incorporate labor saving and quality control efficiencies inherent in its computerized system. Four easily maneuvered tanks of liquid pigment and a computerized system enables one operator to input data for the desired color shade of the concrete, creating an accurate product each time.

Technical assistance is offered in every phase from the use of its products, from the new products which includes concrete imprint stamps, color release agents, dry shake color hardeners, and the liquid metering systems to orders for standard dry pigments. Sales extend throughout the United States, Canada, and other market areas, and have increased to the extent that a second plant is being opened in Rialto, California.

Through the recognition of past and present contributions of its employees to the success of Solomon Colors, the company has become an ESOP Corporation to keep building on the employees' proud tradition of customer service.

Mel-O-Cream Donuts International

A box of donuts from Mel-O-Cream is a familiar sight at breakfast meetings in Springfield. Area residents tend to judge other donuts by Mel-O-Cream's exceptional taste. In 1932, when the first Mel-O-Cream shop opened in Springfield, the glazed, yeast-raised donut was introduced to the community. Six months later Kelly Grant, Sr. purchased the shop and a Springfield tradition began to grow. A secret formula involved in that purchase, was in the cream part of the doughnut mixture. The recipe for the "cream base"-the eggs, sugar, shortening, flavorings, and incredibly, mashed potatoes remain a trade secret. Potato flour, developed during World War II, meant that suddenly the labor intensive peeling and mashing of potatoes was no longer required. That was a task no one missed or remembers fondly. The glazed donut remains the highest volume seller even though up to 40 additional varieties of yeast, cake doughnuts, and French crullers are offered today.

Grant sold donuts in both retail and wholesale markets with a number of ups and downs during the Great Depression, World War II, and changes in nutrition. In 1954 his son, Kelly Grant, Jr. purchased the business. Grant Sr., however, enjoyed remaining active in the retail business until he was in his 80s. Under Grant Jr. the business grew from the one retail store to 14 franchises and advanced into an interstate wholesale market.

Mel-O-Cream Donuts International, Inc., while no longer in the franchise business, continues to supply the remaining franchises with its products. Today, the Mel-O-Cream focus is on its frozen-preformed dough and prefried products brokered in an eleven-state area.

The company handles its own product shipping, all of which are Kosher-Dairy certified, using its own trucks and special packaging to ensure on-time arrival and convenience to the supermarket bakeries, industrial cafeteria and food services using its products. Continued growth lead to construction of a new 68,000-square-foot facility on 18 acres of land in western Springfield. There is now more flexible use of space for added products and room for future expansion. Frozen formed yeast dough for breads, dinner rolls, and buns are new areas of production for the company and becoming an increasing market. The prefried frozen donut line has grown greatly in popularity surpassing the frozen yeast donut line. The prefried product requires less training and time at the customer's site over that needed by the frozen yeast dough.

Customer demand dictates when new or special request donut varieties are added or removed. Over eight million dozen donuts sold every year testify to Mel-O-Cream's exceptional quality and no fudging on ingredients policy that continues as a company standard. The Mel-O-Cream Donut is more than just a vehicle for icing or filling, its taste stands on its own, and it remains a Springfield original.

The 68,000-square-foot Mel-O-Cream Donuts Production Facility, located on Springfield's far west side was completed in September of 1997.

Mel-O-Cream President Kelly A. Grant, Jr. (left) and Vice President David W. Waltrip (right) show of a case of pre-fried donuts.

Phoenix International

The Springfield, Illinois plant plays an important role in company innovation and production.

The global positioning system (GPS) that adjusts the right amount of nitrogen distributed to specific areas of a farmer's field, the automatic opening of irrigation valves, the coffee-maker that brews the morning cup of coffee—all can trace their circuit boards to Phoenix International, a leader in the field of custom design and manufacture of electronic SYSTEMS for original equipment manufacturers. The company made a name for itself in ruggedly durable electronic assemblies placed in heavy construction equipment designed to handle the jostling and environmental conditions found in the road and building industries. But the diversity of electronic applications produced today is keeping the company strong and growing.

While headquartered in Fargo, North Dakota, the Springfield, Illinois plant plays an important role in company innovation and production. Illini Technology (established in Springfield in 1983) merged with Phoenix International in 1996 and, Phoenix became a part of John Deere in 1999. Deere now looks to Phoenix to keep it on the cutting edge of technology.

A new 87,000-square-foot building in Springfield has been designed with the specific requirements for the assembly of electronic circuit boards. This includes special flooring for electrostatic discharge (ESD), a climate-controlled environment, state-of-the-art equipment—much of it is automated for precision accuracy—as well as space for design, testing, and shipping and room for growth.

To stay competitive Phoenix also takes a special interest in their employees, providing a stimulating workplace environment and offering one of the best benefit packages around. Electronic engineers make up approximately forty percent of the workforce. With this percentage, it is apparent new technology is where Phoenix International excels. Original equipment manufacturers (OEM) approach Phoenix with a concept or an expression of their need. Phoenix then works to design the appropriate integrated or integrated with mechanical solutions required. Electronic components may be for embedded controls in an engine, circuitry needs in a fiber optics situation, or for display boards receiving satellite signals. The engineering team analyzes and controls the management of time lines, cost constraints, research, development, testing under a variety of physical conditions, and the manufacturing of electronics. They collaborate with a network of experts related to the product in which the circuit boards will be placed. Service warranty and technical assistance at the installation site are included. Customers with build-to-print-requests (electronic designs ready for manufacture) also contract with Phoenix. Continual cost analysis reviews help both the client and Phoenix share in savings from new procedures.

Quality engineers, dedicated staff, and efficient product development and production procedures have provided Phoenix with a strong base of clients. With the projections of a doubling of business over the next five years and once again in the following five, Phoenix International looks to a bright future.

Phoenix International is a leader in the field of custom design and manufacture of electronic SYSTEMS for original equipment manufacturers.

Photo by Terry Farmer

Springfield **123**

chapter | **eleven**

11

BUSINESS, FINANCE & THE PROFESSIONS

Express Personnel Services, 124-125
The Greater Springfield Chamber of Commerce, 126-127
Kerber, Eck & Braeckel LLP, 128-129
Sorling, Northrup, Hanna, Cullen and Cochran, Ltd., 130-131
Hanson Professional Services Inc., 132-133
Staab Funeral Home, 134
Resource One, 135
HIP Advertising, 136
Illinois National Bank, 137
Kirlin-Egan & Butler Funeral Home and
   Cremation Tribute Center, 138
Standard Mutual Insurance Company, 139
The Horace Mann Companies, 140
Systemax Corporation, 141

Photo by Terry Farmer

Express Personnel Services

It is a win win situation at Express Personnel where both job seekers and business clients find success. "The approach involves a professional evaluation of the customer's needs and wants," says franchise owner Jim Britton. Express Personnel's certified professionals learn as much as they can about the client business including their standards, business personality, expectations of employees, the skills needed, the demands of the job, and so on. Express also learns as much as they can about the job seekers, determining their employment needs, expectations, training, and skills. The match can then be made.

Husband and wife, Jim and Carole Britton have been in the staffing business since 1980. They became a part of the Express Personnel franchise in 1986 and have offices in both Springfield and Bloomington. Raised in Springfield, the Brittons have developed an intimate knowledge of the community they serve. This vested interest shows in the commitment and dedication they put into their work. They began in a 660-square-foot, windowless office. In 1990 they moved to a 3000 square foot space and then added another 3000 square feet expecting that to last a lifetime. In January of 2001 they moved into a new, custom designed building at 3000 Professional Drive in Park South and are utilizing 15,000 square feet of space.

Recognizing and adapting to societal changes affecting employment has been important in the growth of this business. No longer does the average employee expect to stay with one company throughout their lifetime nor do companies now commonly offer that kind of job security. Rapid changes in technology as well as acquisitions and mergers keep many employers and employees in flux. Many employees are on the lookout for new challenges and variety in their work. Personnel services have become an important way for both the employers and employees to adapt to these changes.

Jim and Carole Britton, Franchise owners. Photo by Terry Farmer

Express Personnel offers options in a diverse range of situations. Some job seekers prefer temporary or contract employment. Many of these people become career associates with Express Personnel and qualify for medical, retirement, vacation, and other benefits. They have many choices in the jobs they accept including full time or part time hours. They gain a broad base of experience and meet new people creating friendships, contacts, and future employment opportunities.

A career change may be the goal of other job seekers. Express does the homework, saving much valuable time that might otherwise be spent looking through ads and knocking on doors. For the employer, Express does the screening and initial interviewing. A direct job placement may be the result. Sometimes, though, an evaluation hire option is the best approach. In this situation both the employer and employee have the opportunity to evaluate each other while on the job determining whether a situation is right for a more permanent full-time hire.

Express Personnel offers businesses a full range of staffing services covering a wide spectrum of types of

The Brittons and their local staff. Photo by Terry Farmer

Express Regional Headquarters for Illinois and Indiana. 3000 Professional Drive, Springfield, Illinois. Photo by Terry Farmer

employees including Sales, Accounting, Office, Customer Care, Labor, and Industrial workers. "We have become the way that companies acquire their workforce, whether they need to hire employees or want to utilize temporary staffing," according to Jim Britton. A number of employers no longer maintain their own personnel departments but depend upon the professionals at Express Personnel to keep them fully staffed.

Express gives support and stability to the business community by providing contract or temporary workers at peak times thus reducing the risk of future layoffs. These workers are not dependent upon one company for work but instead look to Express for ongoing employment. An Express career associate can be fully employed year round while receiving benefits.

When layoffs do occur at a client company, Express Personnel can provide workshops for that client's employees providing advice on updating resumes, guidance on how to secure new employment, and insight into opportunities available in the job market.

Express Services, Inc. has recognized the Brittons with numerous awards for their sales and service. The Gordon Blair Heritage Award is particularly special to the Brittons because it is "presented to an individual or individuals possessing extraordinary enthusiasm, positive attitude, and integrity that has had a profound influence on the overall success and future growth of Express Personnel Services." Jim Britton also serves as a regional developer of Express Personnel Services Franchise Company with responsibilities for developing Express offices throughout Illinois and Indiana.

The Brittons and their five-year "plus" employees. Photo by Terry Farmer

It is with a sincere dedication towards helping people that Express Personnel operates. The longevity of their own employees speaks to the job satisfaction felt in providing staffing solutions. The Brittons and their 40 staffing professionals fill over 4,800 positions each year. When asked to what they attribute the extraordinary success of their Express offices, Jim and Carole say, "that's simple, it's our great staff, they have a tremendous commitment to helping people succeed."

The Greater Springfield Chamber of Commerce

The Chamber's headquarters (above) are located at 3 South Old Capitol Plaza in Springfield's historic central business district, two doors west of the law office of Abraham Lincoln. This central location is only a few blocks from the State Capitol (right) and the community's major financial and tourist areas. Photos by Terry Farmer

The Greater Springfield Chamber of Commerce has a distinguished history, a vital presence, and a bright future in Springfield's business and economic life. The Chamber is an active partner in promoting a stronger business climate and civic improvements in the Springfield area. From aggressively seeking to locate new firms in Sangamon County to taking an active role in solving the problem of a future water supply, the Chamber is at the forefront of change in the community.

In the years after the Civil War, America was entering an era of unprecedented industrial and business growth. Reflective of that change, Springfield community leaders formed a Board of Trade in 1869 to promote business and commerce and encourage manufacturing and industry. That organization, although not a direct ancestor to today's Chamber, was the inspiration for later, similar groups, from the Merchants and Shippers Association to Springfield Commercial Association, which eventually merged to form the Chamber.

The Springfield chamber was formed in 1953 as the Springfield Association of Commerce and Industry. Its current name was adopted in 1970 and its purpose is essentially the same as the original Board of Trade—to promote economic growth and betterment of Springfield's Capital. Recognizing that Springfield and Sangamon County are linked as one business community, the chamber's mission is to enhance the area's business climate and to promote and stimulate orderly economic growth in Sangamon County and environs for the benefit of the members and the community.

With more than 1,450 member organizations, the Greater Springfield Chamber of Commerce is the largest chamber organization in downstate Illinois. It has a 13-member staff and is governed by a 21-member Board of Directors. The staff and board represent only a small portion of the local people involved with Chamber activities and promotion. More than 300 volunteers serve on the Chamber's fifteen standing and ad hoc committees including Agribusiness, Ambassadors, Technology, Drug Free Workplace, Workforce and Education, Government Affairs, Healthcare, Infrastructure, Leadership Springfield, Public Relations, Plae Dae, and Small Business Council.

Two of the more widely known programs of the Chamber are Leadership Springfield and Plae Dae activities. Leadership Springfield taps the rich vein of potential community leaders employed in local business and government and offers a nine-month course of intensive exploration of community leadership, problem solving, and organizational practices. Participants are required to identify and solve a problem for a local organization before completing the course. Plae Dae, which started in 1948 at a local farm as an "informal summer outing for business firm leaders," has since moved to Lake Springfield. This annual event has become a popular golf outing and picnic and is a major fundraiser for the Chamber. Additionally the objectives of the Chamber are further carried out through the Economic Development

Council (EDC). The Chamber has partnered with the City of Springfield and Sangamon County in this joint venture. The EDC serves as the leading economic development agency in the county. The Council's primary goals are to attract new businesses to Sangamon County and to assist and encourage the expansion of local business firms. Through pooling resources with government and business, the Chamber has leveraged its resources and is able to promote growth in a wider area than would be possible alone.

Chamber staff regularly visit local firms to assess their needs and those of the business community generally and to identify ways to mobilize technical assistance to facilitate job growth.

Chamber presence in local government decision-making is vitally important. Chamber leaders spoke out forcefully and publicly, for example, in favor of a second lake for the region and the Chamber has been a key element in the effort to secure high quality air service for Springfield. Members turn to the Chamber for knowledge and skills to enhance their performance and productivity. The Chamber is also a source of community information for tourists and businesses for everything from what to see to specifics on local economic climate.

The Greater Springfield Chamber of Commerce disseminates a wealth of information through its publications. The *Membership Directory and Buyer's Guide* lists chamber members alphabetically and categorizes them by product and services. *Trends* provide up-to-date demographic information on the Springfield area including useful statistics on population, labor force, and retail sales. Over 200 manufacturing firms are listed in the *Manufacts* publication.

The Chamber's Program of Action is a reminder of what staff does everyday to help their membership and local business community by:
• Growing the economy
• Informing, educating, and assisting the membership
• Promoting members and their products and services
• Enhancing the workforce and leadership base
• Shaping the local business climate

The spirit of the Chamber was summed up in a history of the organization: "It was in the course of making Springfield 'a good product' that the Chamber and its predecessors had exerted perhaps the greatest and most lasting effect on the community. From the formation of the Sanitary District to the construction of Lake Springfield, from construction of Veterans Parkway to railroad relocation, from the building of Capital Airport to the opening of Sangamon State University and its merger with the University of Illinois, Springfield's business associations for a hundred years have been working (in the words of the Chambers 1920 constitution) 'to promote the economic, civic, and social welfare of the people of Springfield, Illinois and vicinity.'"

Active involvement in the local community means the Greater Springfield Chamber of Commerce can, in its own words, provide "leadership and synergy which enables its members to accomplish collectively what they cannot do individually."

The view from the Chamber's Office features the historic Illinois Old State Capitol. Photo by Terry Farmer

Lake Springfield serves the community in several ways as a source of: drinking water, cooling water for the city-owned and operated electric generating facility, and numerous recreational and park assets. Photo by Terry Farmer

Kerber, Eck & Braeckel LLP

One of the top 100 accounting firms in the United States, based on revenue, is headquartered in Springfield—Kerber, Eck & Braeckel LLP (KEB). Founded in 1931 by Louis J. Kerber and Albert O. Eck Sr., two certified public accountants (CPAs), who opened offices in Springfield, Illinois and St. Louis, Missouri. In 1938 Walter E. Braeckel joined the firm, establishing the name that continues today. Offices were subsequently added in Belleville and Carbondale, Illinois, Cape Girardeau, Missouri, and Milwaukee, Wisconsin. KEB has 18 partners and two principals, 11 of whom reside in the Springfield office.

KEB is a full-service regional accounting and consulting firm. It consists of professional experts serving a host of clients nationwide; from individuals to large corporations, businesses to not-for-profit organizations. Each of its clients has personal, business, and organizational objectives. To help them reach their goals, KEB provides a full range of auditing and accounting, tax, and management consulting services. Efforts are coordinated to provide each client with the finest professional services in a timely and personalized manner.

KEB believes clients gain distinct advantages from its size. The Springfield office is the largest accounting office in Springfield and has grown to over 70 professionals and support staff. One of KEB's strengths is its commitment to providing its people with the tools and training they need to best serve their clients. The professional staff offers a breadth of experience suited to almost any client needs, yet they remain small enough to offer clients personal service in hopes of a long-term relationship. According to Daniel Cadigan, the firm's managing partner, "We couple personal service with professional excellence—an integral part of our philosophy—and this gives us a distinct competitive edge. We commit our total resources to help our clients achieve greater success and profitability. Because when our clients are successful, we are too."

A professional firm is only as good as its individual members. Each member of the KEB team is genuinely concerned about its clients. To effectively serve industry and specific needs, specialized knowledge and skills are needed. The KEB team knows that trained skilled professionals with sincere client interest will serve its customers best. Therefore, they recruit only those people whose commitment matches their own. Training and continuing professional education is vital to provide professional excellence and they believe this distinguishes them from other organizations. KEB provides value-added services and the compelling evidence of this is the rapid growth the firm has experienced.

KEB was founded on the principles of providing accounting, auditing, general business advice, and tax planning and preparation services. According to Dale Becker, partner-in-charge of the Springfield office, "Our key to success is to focus on the three 'Rs'—relationships, resources, and results. We build relationships with our clients and use our resources to provide results, which are value-added services for our clients."

KEB provides a full-range of accounting services—from the more routine services such as compilations, general bookkeeping, sales tax return preparation, payroll processing, and payroll tax return preparation to the more non-routine services such as reviews and audits. KEB's review and auditing services provide assurance of their clients' financial information. Providing high-quality

From left to right—Stephen L. Povse, Dale M. Becker, Deborah J. Ringer, and J. Marc Carter. Photo by Terry Farmer

From left to right—Daniel W. Cadigan, Denis Moja, Skip Hedger, and Cheryl J. Martin. Photo by Terry Farmer

services in a timely manner are part of KEB's long tradition and history, but they also believe in gaining a solid understanding of the client's business and directing the process so that it becomes a valuable foundation for developing tax and business strategies.

KEB is also well known for its tax preparation services. However, they offer more than efficient and accurate tax return preparation. Tax law revisions and new regulations have profound effects on their clients. KEB devotes considerable time to remain abreast of tax law changes as they occur. According to David Burnett, a tax partner, "Careful planning is the key to effective tax management. Many times there are several ways to handle a given situation, each with different tax and financial implications. We analyze each alternative to help our clients make the best choice."

Over the years, other services were added in order for KEB to meet the changing needs of their clients. KEB provides management consulting, asset management services, and information technology consulting. KEB's management consulting department has proven they see beyond the obvious. KEB provides much more than just financial-related consulting. They have successfully expanded into non-financial consulting. "We examine symptoms of poor performance and get to the heart of underlying problems. We make an objective analysis of your situation and provide specific recommendations for improving performance and profitability," according to Skip Hedger, management consulting principal. KEB's management consulting department has provided businesses and governmental agencies with strategic planning, management reviews, organizational analysis, operational reviews, performance measurement systems, business valuations, and much more.

In 1998, KEB added asset management services. KEB wanted to take advantage of its strong business knowledge and provide investment advisory and asset management services to many of the entrusted accounting relationships that have existed over the past 70 years. KEB has adopted a theory supported by the world's leading financial economists, three of whom received a Nobel Prize for their contributions. These economists conducted ongoing research resulting in the formation of the Modern Portfolio Theory. KEB has adopted this theory. Marc Carter, a partner and Registered Investment Advisor says, "In light of all the statistical data indicating the critical significance of asset class selection, we strongly believe that Modern Portfolio Theory and passive asset class investing is the best way for us to develop prudent, long-term portfolios for our clients".

The firm also provides Information Technology (IT) consulting to many of its clients. As an outgrowth of its accounting services, KEB has offered IT consulting related to accounting software systems for over 15 years. KEB is a registered reseller and support office for Mas90 and also provides support for QuickBooks. Mas90 has continued to be regarded as one of the leading mid-market accounting software programs. KEB also provides network support for Microsoft platforms and performs systems design and installation related to network infrastructure.

KEB has a long tradition of quality service over the past 70 years. A portion of the KEB mission statement summarizes its philosophy. "At KEB, we are committed to fully serving your needs. We are CPAs, management consultants, and business advisors who promise you professional, personalized service." KEB looks forward to continuing its proud tradition of excellence into the 21st century.

From left to right—Joe Alessandrini, Nan K. Hendrickson, and David W. Burnett. Photo by Terry Farmer

Sorling, Northrup, Hanna, Cullen and Cochran, Ltd.

Sorling has a team of full-time lawyer-lobbyists present at every session of the Illinois General Assembly.

You never know when you might need an attorney, for any of a thousand reasons. In Sorling, Northrup, Hanna, Cullen and Cochran Ltd., Springfield has the best of two worlds—comprehensive legal services normally found in a large metropolitan law office and the attentiveness and timeliness of a small firm. Carl Sorling, the founder of the firm patterned the organization after those in large cities. Rather than specializing in one area of law, he assembled lawyers from different disciplines, creating a firm that could provide legal service for any of the varied legal issues that might confront a client.

Carl A. Sorling was a young Chicago lawyer in the 1920s when he joined the former Springfield Marine Bank as their in-house attorney. He soon took advantage of an opportunity to become an independent attorney and still continue his work with the bank. As his law practice grew, Sorling partnered with B. Lacey Catron and John H. Hardin in 1945. By 1975 the firm's name had changed to reflect the then partners—Carl A. Sorling, Charles J. Northrup, Phillip E. Hanna, George W. Cullen, and Thomas L. Cochran. Northrup specialized in property law, Hanna in tax and estate planning, Cullen was a trial attorney, and Cochran a corporate and transactions attorney. Today the firm has 35 lawyers with 22 of them as shareholders (partners) representing a comprehensive range of expertise in legal disciplines.

Each of the firm's lawyers serves in one or more of four practice groups- personal services, litigation, business, and government services. Having an in-house expert to provide timely advice and legal support to clients is the firm's foremost goal. It also gives the firm the capability to team subject specialists in handling highly complex and sophisticated cases.

The personal services practice group deals with issues faced by individuals and families, such as wills, estate planning, trusts, taxes, and property sales. The trial lawyers in the litigation group are on the front lines in court or before arbitrators almost daily. The business services practice group addresses a spectrum of issues regarding the establishment, management, and dissolution of business entities. Clients range from small family businesses to large conglomerates. The government practice group represents private businesses before government; represents government bodies—school boards, municipalities, state universities; works with individuals and groups on election matters; and comprehensively lobbies the Illinois General Assembly and executive branch.

Technology plays a very important role in providing efficient, quality client service at Sorling. Full text client case files are stored in a database giving the attorney quick access to older documents while the client is visiting, eliminating the need for a second appointment to allow for retrieval of stored paper copies. (Client files can only be accessed in-house and are protected by several security systems). The firm operates an extensive Web site, and distributes a newsletter by electronic mail.

Firm attorneys regularly provide legal services required by business managers and property owners.

Sorling serves the public utility community, including electric, gas, telecommunications, and water businesses.

An electronic conflict identification program cross-references client information quickly to identify any potential client conflicts of interest. If there are, it is immediately brought to the attention of both parties to discuss direction. Loyalty to clients has always been a part of the code of conduct at the firm and that has included avoiding representing clients with conflicting interests.

A number of public databases give the lawyer an instantaneous check on the status of court litigation and legislative matters. The extensive law library is also right at the lawyer's fingertips from a personal computer at each attorney's desk. No more is there the time-consuming, tedious thumbing through pages of text to find needed information. Clients recognize and appreciate the economy and convenience. Litigation documentation systems are maintained with state-of-the-art capabilities ranging from the cataloging and accessing thousands of evidentiary documents to three-dimensional modeling, that might be used, for instance, in visualizing the dispersion of chemicals over land tracts.

Professional organizations benefit not only from memberships by Sorling attorneys, but also through the time given authoring articles, handbooks, and lecturing at professional gatherings, sharing the experiences and knowledge they've gained. Educational speaking engagements in classrooms and at clubs and organization meetings, as well as the personal time to serve on Springfield area community boards, committees, and volunteer events are also a part of life at Sorling.

From administrative law to zoning, and all the disciplines in-between, the Sorling, Northrup, Hanna, Cullen, and Cochran Ltd. law offices have fulfilled founder Carl Sorling's most ambitious dreams of a major law firm able to hand a wide variety of legal challenges.

Firm litigators regularly practice before state and federal courts.

Hanson Professional Services Inc.

Hanson Professional Services Inc.'s impressive growth is a direct result of its dedication to serving its clientele. Through a series of mergers and acquisitions, Hanson has expanded to offer a full range of architectural, engineering, scientific, and program management services.

Hanson began in November of 1954 when Walter Hanson and two other engineers formed a partnership specializing in bridge design and structural engineering. The three rented a small, second-floor office at 401 E. Capitol in Springfield, Illinois, rolled up their sleeves, and got to work.

A Firm Foundation

Work was slow at first. The fledgling firm, then called Walter E. Hanson and Associates, logged 40 jobs in 1955, its first full year of operation. Most of those jobs were bridge and structural projects on the Kansas Turnpike. Soon, however, they expanded beyond structural engineering to include more broad-based civil engineering projects and work on soil mechanics and foundation engineering.

A National Company, a Local Mainstay

From its small beginnings in 1954, Hanson has grown into a national employee-owned consulting firm employing 370 people in 14 offices nationwide. Corporate headquarters are located at 1525 South Sixth Street in Springfield.

The firm still retains a strong spirit of camaraderie among its professionals, many of whom have been around for decades.

Sergio "Satch" Pecori, president and chief executive officer, worked his way up at Hanson. After receiving his bachelor's and master's degrees from the University of Illinois in the mid-1970s, he joined the staff full time. He was named president in 1998 and chief executive officer in 1999.

The Millennium Center, on the main campus of Lincoln Land Community College in Springfield, provides state-of-the-art technology for educational programs and offices.

He has seen the firm grow, as well as its mission.

"Today, our mission is to help our clients meet their customers' needs," says Pecori. "We help them achieve a competitive advantage, and we provide a wide range of services to accomplish this. We are involved in many projects from conception to completion. We can help clients obtain funding, site facilities, purchase land, and design and build facilities through our design-build delivery process. And we're involved with facilities management, maintenance, and operations."

"As our company continues to branch out into new markets, we often face the challenge of letting our clients, as well as prospective clients, know that we provide more than just engineering services," Pecori says, noting that Hanson has acquired four companies since 1993, adding architectural, mechanical, electrical, and telecommunication services.

Yet despite its national presence and focus, Hanson provides a powerful benefit to the local economy as well.

Hanson's economic impact is evidenced by figures taken from an economic impact analysis conducted by Michael Ayers, Ph.D., chief operating officer for the Illinois Chamber of Commerce. Based on Hanson's fiscal year 2000 income, expenditure, and employment data, "Hanson helps sustain an estimated 850 jobs locally and generates more than $25.7 million in business within the area," Ayers says.

From the firm's professionals working in the field to the staff working behind the scenes, Hanson is committed to tailoring solutions that work. Some of those solutions are highly visible, like the Clark Bridge near St. Louis, Missouri. Hanson designed the spectacular $92 million bridge. It was the first in the

The award-winning Clark Bridge over the Mississippi River near Alton, Illinois, has become an area landmark. It is one of the first three-span, cable-stayed, single pylon common saddle bridges in the United States. The design makes the bridge striking in appearance and improves its resistance to seismic forces.

United States to feature a combination of dual-plane cable stays supported by single pylons. The firm's innovative design work on the bridge won several awards, including the recent Federal Design Achievement Award from the National Endowment for the Arts and the U.S. General Services Administration. The entry was one of 35 winning projects out of a national field of 338 submissions. The awards are given every four years.

Hanson's touch reaches across the world. On a tropical island in the Pacific, Hanson designed a radio broadcast station. The station supplements Voice of America broadcasts from the Philippine Islands and Thailand, improving coverage to China, Indonesia, and the western Pacific. Working with the United States Information Agency, Hanson also designed a transmitter and administration building, an operations area, antenna field, and power plant at the 800-acre site.

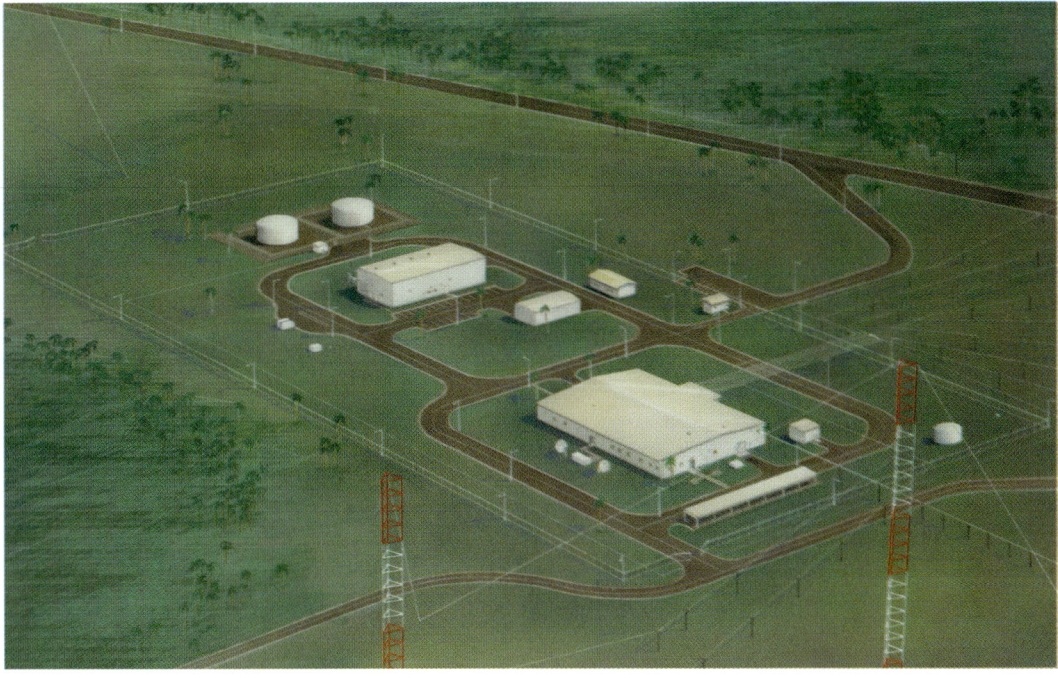

Working for the International Broadcasting Bureau, Hanson designed and provided systems integration for this Voice of America radio relay station on the remote island of Sao Tome, West Africa. The station makes it possible to air programs in Africa and the Middle East.

As Hanson's services and client based have expanded over the years, its corporate image has changed. This growth is reflected in the recent name change from Hanson Engineers to Hanson Professional Services Inc.

An example of the expanded services is seen in the $7.1 million land acquisition and program management contract Hanson won for the South Suburban Airport in the Chicago area.

An Award-Winning Firm

Important design projects in recent years include the Burlington Northern Santa Fe Railway Co.-United Parcel Service Intermodal Facility in Hodgkins, Illinois, the largest facility of its kind in the United States, devoted to rerouting train cargo; the National Storage Tank Administration Program for AT&T, a nationwide program for retiring underground storage tanks; the $148 million low-level radioactive waste cleanup being conducted for the Illinois Department of Nuclear Safety at a site owned by Kerr-McGee Inc. in West Chicago, Illinois; and an award-winning seismic retrofit at an Ameritech switching station in southern Illinois; a contract to perform railroad services worldwide for the U.S. Army Corps of Engineers; and several major bridge and roadway studies for Illinois, Missouri, Indiana, and Iowa.

For the past 14 years, Hanson has consistently appeared in the ENR Top 500-*Engineering News-Record* magazine's listing of premiere design firms in the United States. Hanson recently came in at No. 191 on the national list. The firm was also named one of the fastest-growing architectural/engineering consulting firms in the country, ranking No. 83 as a Zweig Letter Hot Firm for 2001. This ranking is based on a composite of percentage growth and dollar growth in revenue. Hanson also received the coveted 2001 National Society of Professional Engineers' Professional Development Award, which honors employers of engineers who have made outstanding contributions to the advancement and improvement of the engineering profession. Additionally, the firm was named one of the top 25 in the national *CE News* Best Civil Engineering Firms to Work For contest.

Hanson's John Coombe, executive vice president and chief operating officer; Bob Cusick, executive vice president and chief technical officer; and Satch Pecori, president and chief executive officer, visit a section of the Stanford Avenue under construction. The new east-west corridor will improve traffic flow and provide a grade separation at a busy railroad corridor.

Staab Funeral Home

Second and third generation Staab family members continue to build traditions through their personalized service. Left to right standing: Mark, Jean, Suanne Staab Palazzolo, and Paul II. Seated: Vincent, Catherine, and George Staab, Jr.

Holding balloon releases, displaying family memorabilia and photos, or playing favorite pieces of music (perhaps on a piano rather than the organ) are personal choices families make when honoring the memory, celebrating the life of, and grieving for their deceased. "Personalization of service" is the key term in the funeral profession today, but it is something the Staab family has offered for over three quarters of a century. When George J. Staab and John H. O'Donnell established the O'Donnell and Staab Funeral Home in 1927, the needs of families from varying religious traditions and cultural backgrounds were given special attention. Three generations of the Staab family have since kept personalization as a goal. The ceremony of life has been and continues to be a sacred event says Suanne Staab Palazzolo.

In 1937 George Staab and his wife, Christine, chose a beautiful Victorian house built in 1873 at 1109 S. Fifth Street, both for their residence and for the home of Staab Funeral Home. George is especially remembered in the community for his compassion, commitment, and willingness to help those in need. He began a tradition that continues today of accommodating all families regardless of financial circumstances. The reason, according to Mark Staab, is because of the high regard for the sanctity of human life which is a major part of the culture at Staab.

The Staab house, while having undergone three different expansions, retains its comfortable, home-like atmosphere. Soothing colors and tasteful décor greet guests throughout the five visitation rooms, offices, and client family lounge. Staab's funeral coaches are garaged in a restored carriage house at the rear of the property. The horse-drawn carriage of an earlier day was replaced with Staab's combination ambulance/funeral vehicles. It was common into the 1960s and earlier for funeral homes to provide ambulance service in a community. P.J. Staab II considers the Staab complex a landmark of service and history.

Pre-planning with payment options, designed to lessen the burden on a bereaved family, are a growing part of client service. For the living, an array of books, brochures and referrals for counseling or other needs are available. These services express the Staab family's compassion for clients, reaching far beyond the immediate time of a family member's death. Twice each year, services of remembrance are held, open to anyone in the community. One, on or near the 4th of July, honors military veterans. The second, is held during the Christmas season, traditionally a difficult time for those who have lost a loved one.

The Staab family members feel a special responsibility to the Springfield area and take an active role in a variety of organizations. There is little wonder that Staab Funeral Home ranks in the top percentage nationally for the number of families served each year.

The historic 19th century house that serves as the Staab Funeral Home has been tastefully decorated with the thought of making families feel comfortable and at home.

Resource One

Resource One's corporate office at Fourth and Adams is recognized as one of the most innovative office furniture showrooms in the United States. Photo by Terry Farmer

At Resource One each client's situation is viewed as unique and so is every solution. There are no cookie-cutter approaches. For office solutions, this firm is the one resource center a customer needs to find virtually all of their furniture, panels, filing and storage systems, wire management systems, lighting, accessories, flooring, wall coverings, etc. to establish an efficient and comfortable workspace. At Resource One, experienced, professional staff work with over 300 product lines and the countless options each company offers. Names such as Knoll, Allsteel, Hon, and Paoli allow the customer to become familiar with the best solutions available as well as the ones that meet their immediate needs. With so many decisions to be made, the space planners, interior designers, and project managers collaborate to tailor these choices to the customer's setting and provide visual walk-throughs with Auto-Cad software and actual samples.

Today's offices have varied work configurations. Team approaches may require workstations that surround a central teaming area. Conference tables may be triangularly shaped if teleconferencing is a part of the communication system. Lounge chairs with a tablet-arm for the lap top, a cup holder, and drawer under the chair, have replaced the conference table in some instances. Competition for the trend-setting Generation-X employee has created a demand for offices with high-tech appearance and maybe a bit of fun in the colors, textures, and accessories. Resource One is abreast of all of these shifts in the corporate world. Its services also accommodate many non-office situations as well—restaurants, common areas in high-rises, hospitals, schools—anywhere seating, tables, carpeting, etc. are needed, by individual consumers or large organizations.

When Cindy Davis established Resource One in 1987 with a partner and one employee, she had a clear vision based on experience of services an office solutions business should provide. Today, nearly 30 employees design and furnish the total work environment with concern for ergonomics and safety issues, whether they are called in as consultants or involved in the complete design of the workplace from space planning, to interior design, through installation. Cindy Davis and now partner, Craig Mannschreck, along with Cindy's husband Larry Davis, (professionally a nurse anesthetist and a management officer in the firm), have built a business that reaches across the United States. With Cindy as majority owner, the firm is a Certified Minority and Female Business Enterprise with the state of Illinois. The principals are firm supporters of downtown Springfield, community service activities, as well as the organizations in their industry such as the Office Furniture Dealer Alliance and Central Illinois chapters of A.I.A. and I.F.M.A.

Enthusiasm and energy, plus pride in their accomplishments has created a large customer base for the Resource One team—a formula sure to spell success.

The reception station at Marine Bank in Springfield —a Resource One project.

HIP Advertising

When two grade school/high school friends get together to form a business partnership and still remain friends, it's a good indication they know how to cooperate, communicate, and compromise. Add talent, enthusiasm, and genuine concern for producing a quality product and the result is an award-winning advertising and marketing firm. The two friends gained experience, one in Chicago, the other in Springfield, before founding HIP Advertising in 1993. Myra L. Hoffman and Barb Pape Frankenstein have brought a new level of creativity to the Springfield marketplace ever since.

Shortly after starting the company, the public quickly took note and so did the advertising world. Just one look at the fireplace mantle in HIP's headquarters, and the capabilities of this firm become apparent. The mantle is filled with ADDY® Awards, the American Advertising Federation's measure of creative excellence. These awards include several Best of Show as well as the Judge's Award for Excellence. HIP has also won the Telly Award, a highly respected national competition honoring outstanding television commercials, video production, and films.

HIP serves clients on both the local, national, and international level, with a single promotional need all the way to a multi-media campaign. Services run the gamut from radio and television spots, to brochures, direct mail pieces, Web sites, videos, corporate identity packages, print ads, and trade show exhibits, as well as media planning and buying.

Accounts range from business to business marketing, to retail and consumer advertising, to not-for-profit organizations, and public service groups. An in-depth study of a client's business or organization to help determine marketing objectives is an important first step in developing a new relationship with a client. From there, HIP works with the client to determine the best strategy to fit their particular needs and budget.

Besides the principals, HIP Advertising employs some of the area's most talented advertising and marketing professionals. A team approach is taken on every account, with the entire staff sitting down to brainstorm a new campaign and to share ideas from their individual departments. The agency has worked diligently over the years to cultivate a roster of high-quality resources for outside services including photography, printing, and audio/video production.

"HIP Advertising is professional, courteous, creative, enthusiastic, and simply fun to work with," says one local client in praise. HIP has created an impressive niche in the Springfield community and continually seeks new challenges in the quest to offer their client's ongoing success.

Outstanding in their field (from left to right): Beth Camplain, Linda Voorhees, Melissa Rigg, Steve Curry, Myra Hoffman, Sarah Petty, Barb Pape Frankenstein, and Erin Verbeck.

Illinois National Bank

Some things are better the second time around, and Illinois National Bank in Springfield is one of them. A series of bank mergers and acquisitions in the late 1990s led to the near extinction of locally owned banks. Illinois National Bank, with over 100 years of service, was one of the casualties of that era.

Recognizing a void, a group of local investors and former Illinois National Bank employees set about forming a new, locally-owned financial institution. Illinois National Bank (INB) opened its doors for the second time on June 21, 1999. Under the leadership of Richard K. McCord, James V. Antonacci, and the late Linda Culver, INB promised to bring back a traditional high level of banking service and responsiveness to the Springfield market.

Just getting the doors open was a task that required the entire staff to pull together as a team. Its former owner vacated the new INB location at the corner of 4th and Capitol Avenue only two days prior to the bank opening. During those two days you would find the bank president washing windows alongside a teller sweeping the floor. The equal sharing of the workload then has given the staff a sense of unity that has permeated throughout the operation, and which translates to customers as a friendly, cooperative atmosphere in which to do business

INB hit the ground running, as it re-entered the Springfield market with a strong, experienced staff and a well-capitalized institution. Categorized as a progressive commercial bank, INB is proud of its advanced computer banking technology.

For retail and commercial customers, a click or two on the computer will allow them immediate access to their account information, including images of the front and back of their cancelled checks. There is no longer a need to wait for proof of a cancelled check, nor is there a fee. Customers can have an immediate print record of any such document, all with the click of a mouse. Bank statements can be e-mailed directly to customers for convenience, and state-of-the-art technology keeps information private and secure. New features are certain to be added.

Commercial customers can take advantage of INB's Remittance Processing Center. Once again, state-of-the-art technology enables the Processing Center to receive, track, and deposit payments made to a client business or institution the same day the payment is received. The State of Illinois is one of the Processing Center's largest customers, directing some 5 million transactions through the facility each year. The small business owner, with limited staff, finds the service an equally efficient and accurate way to keep track of accounts.

The City of Springfield has accepted the reincarnation of INB with arms wide open. The success story found at Illinois National Bank proves that when tradition meets financial innovation, great things will happen.

The late Linda Culver, James V. Antonacci, and Richard K. McCord, founding officers of Illinois National Bank, pictured in front of the main branch in 1999.

The original Illinois National Bank (INB) was located on the northeast corner of Fifth and Washington Streets, and served the financial needs of Springfield for over 100 years. INB reopened at 322 East Capitol Avenue (pictured left) in July 1999.

Kirlin-Egan & Butler Funeral Home and Cremation Tribute Center

When Ben Kirlin, a funeral furnisher (undertaker) and Ed Egan, a livery stable owner joined in partnership in 1893 the horse was still necessary to pull the hearse. For over a century Kirlin-Egan & Butler Funeral Home and Cremation Tribute Center has been a family owned and operated business. Their longevity can, in part, be attributed to being continually mindful of changes in social values and attitudes as well as technological changes within their field. Their service offerings before, during, and after funeral ceremonies reflect these changes, as do their up-to-date facilities. Extending genuine support to those grieving is still the primary basis for their outstanding reputation. Kirlin-Egan & Butler's strong record of service has gained membership in the highly regarded International Order of the Golden Rule and the Selected Independent Funeral Homes organizations.

After the deaths of Kirlin and Egan, Mary Kirlin, Ben's daughter operated the funeral home until her death in 1942. At this time, long time employee, Harold Butler purchased the business. Two years after Harold's death in 1963, his nephews, John B. "Jack" Butler and Jerome J. "Jerry" Butler along with Leonard J. Berry and John J. McCarthy acquired the business. Today, Jack Butler, his son Chris, and Jack's sister, Mary Kay Butler-Harrelson continue a tradition of service to people of all faiths and backgrounds.

Responding to a growing number of requests, Kirlin-Egan & Butler recently opened an on-site cremation facility in their willingness to adapt to the changing needs of society. The Cremation Tribute Center provides a place where a private gathering, prayer, and observation of the casket being placed in the cremation chamber can be held for those wishing to have the closure of attending a cremation ceremony (the actual cremation process is not viewed). Realizing, too, the emotional impact pets have on individuals and families, Kirlin-Egan & Butler arranged for a separate cremation area for family animals in the Cremation Tribute Center and have received a very appreciative response to this service.

An open and pleasant service selection room is available for arranging pre-planning details or making at-the-moment funeral arrangements. Personalization of the visitation gathering and funeral ceremonies in ways to commemorate the life of the deceased are encouraged by the Butler family.

Grief is natural and Kirlin-Egan & Butler strives to help people through a healthy grieving process. They are on hand with a caring staff and support services—a certified grief counselor, reading materials on bereavement subjects, follow-up contacts, and a holiday help program. Their comprehensive staff, including licensed professionals, has a respect for life and the lives lost. Chris Butler says a funeral director's work has its share of stress, but knowing the quality of help and support Kirlin-Egan & Butler offers and the appreciation received make the job very satisfying.

Jack Butler, Chris Butler, and Mary Kay Butler Harrelson.

Kirlin-Egan & Butler Funeral Home and Cremation Tribute Center, 900 South 6th Street in Springfield.

Standard Mutual Insurance Company

It was evident that the automobile was here to stay, even though few people owned one in 1921, the year that Frank Roberts established Standard Mutual Insurance Company. During those first years as an automobile insurance company, independent agents sold the policies while Frank and one employee handled the rest of the business. Of course, the number of automobiles increased and, through good management, so did the business. Today, Standard Mutual is a multiple line property and casualty company writing policies throughout Illinois and Indiana, with over $60 million in assets. Continued growth initiated the current home office building with the familiar stately colonial architecture located on South Grand Avenue West at MacArthur Blvd. The company also has offices in Oak Brook, Illinois and Indianapolis, Indiana, and is positioned to expand into other midwestern states.

Standard Mutual Insurance Company's management has continued through three generations. In 1934, Frank Roberts' son, Mark O. Roberts, Sr., joined the firm. He had graduated from the University of Illinois in law, and was a partner in the law firm of Roberts and Kepner. His initial work with his father was to run the Claims Department and handling liability cases for the company while still building his law practice. Mark, Sr. remained active in the legal profession, but took on more of an involvement in the insurance business, becoming president in 1953. His son, Mark O. Roberts, Jr., CPCU, joined the company in 1969 with a degree in insurance and finance from the University of Arkansas, and later obtained an MBA from the University of Illinois. Mark,

Seated left to right: James A. Schultz, CPCU, AU/Senior Vice President, Director; Mrs. Mark O. Roberts, Sr.; and James W. Theis, CPA/Chief Financial Officer, Secretary-Treasurer. Standing left to right: William M. Gibbons, Vice President Claims; Mark O. Roberts, Jr., CPCU/President, Director; and Attorney Hugh J. Graham III, Director. Photo by Terry Farmer

Jr. is the current CEO following his father's retirement in 1992.

Standard Mutual offers complete lines of property and casualty insurance including automobile, liability, homeowners, fire, commercial multi-peril, businessowners, workers' compensation, farm, mobilehome, motorcycle, and inland marine. The company continues to sell its products through professional independent agents. With over 80 years in business, Standard Mutual has consistently been rated "Excellent" by insurance analysts and rating companies.

Standard Mutual's team of employees has seen great changes in the insurance industry, including its state-of-the-art computer operating system serving policyholders and agents quickly and efficiently, plus a 24-hour claims service. Several of the most recent changes at Standard Mutual are a strategic plan to enter additional states and implementation of Ultra Preferred Programs for both Automobile and Homeowners insurance, which carve out competitively priced policies for qualified individuals.

As a home-grown Springfield business, community is important to everyone at Standard Mutual. Its team of employees has been involved in many worthwhile causes including volunteer and employee-sponsored fund raising events, which they select throughout the year. From its beginning, the company's philosophy of providing "quality insurance and personal service" has been a guideline that has served the business well.

Continued growth initiated the current home office building with the familiar stately colonial architecture located on South Grand Avenue West at MacArthur Boulevard. Photo by Terry Farmer

The Horace Mann Companies

At a time when educators had very few benefits, two Springfield teachers—Les Nimmo and Carroll Hall—established the Springfield Credit Union. As they gave auto loans to teachers, they realized many auto owners did not have insurance, so the pair organized the Credit Union Interinsurance Exchange. In 1945, they made an agreement with the Illinois Education Association (IEA) to provide coverage for its members, and they began selling auto insurance.

The original IEA Mutual Insurance Company was later renamed Horace Mann. The name honors the father of American public education and symbolizes the company's commitment to the welfare of the educator community.

As the Springfield-based company expanded, it became attractive to larger businesses. In 1975, The Insurance Company of North America, which later merged to form CIGNA, acquired Horace Mann. Then in August 1989, an investor group that included company management acquired Horace Mann from CIGNA. In November 1991, Horace Mann completed an initial public offering of stock on the New York Stock Exchange.

When it was founded, the company began with three employees headquartered in a second floor office. Now nearly 1,300 home office employees are located in the six-story building built in 1972 and the three-story facility at 100 North Ninth Street leased in 2001. During 2000 and 2001, the home office went through a major remodeling and redecorating project. The extra office space helped consolidate employees who had been scattered in various locations throughout Springfield.

Horace Mann, the largest multiline insurance company focusing on the nation's educators and their families, has an exclusive sales force of nearly 900 agents.

The company's mission has been expanded to provide lifelong financial well-being for educators and their families through personalized service, advice, and a full range of tailored insurance and financial products.

Louis G. Lower II became the president and chief executive officer of Horace Mann in February 2000. Lower's vision for Horace Mann in the 21st century is to dramatically increase growth. "We serve an attractive and growing market," he says. "I take pride in the fact that our business is to take care of educators while they are building the future of our country. As a company founded by educators for educators, our intent is to be the premiere company in meeting their needs."

Horace Mann is one of Springfield's major employers and one of the area's biggest supporters. The company supports local education programs and human services, particularly projects that relate to schools where its participation can make a difference. The company supports programs to build youth leadership, recognize educators for teaching excellence, and promote arts education.

Nearly 1,300 home office employees are located in the six-story building built in 1972.

Horace Mann employees work with each and every client to ensure lifelong financial well-being for its clients.

Systemax Corporation

Systemax corporate headquarters. Photo by Terry Farmer

According to Systemax Corporation founder and president Steve Jackson, a "sincere desire to create products and services that please our clients so much that they freely praise us to others" has been responsible for his company's phenomenal success. What started as a one-man operation in 1982 has grown to become the largest independent company of its kind in the United States, boasting a who's who list of Clients such as the financial services giant, American Express.

Automated teller systems revolutionized the banking industry in the 1970s and '80s, allowing customers, for the first time ever, to access their monies during non-banking hours. ATMs went from a few trial markets to nationwide saturation in only a few years. This phenomenal growth meant demand for consumable products used by the ATMs such as transaction records, deposit envelopes, signage, and other items. At first, the billion dollar corporations who manufacture the teller machines dominated the ATM supply business. They controlled the supply market by guarding the specifications for the products their machines used, making it extremely difficult for anyone else to enter the market. Steve Jackson saw the growth opportunity in this industry and shifted his company's strategic efforts to exclusively focus on it.

Systemax was founded in 1989, seven years after Jackson first started a business designing and selling data processing forms to financial institutions. After first solving a series of product quality issues for a local ATM network, he then went on to develop a production and distribution system that resulted in drastically reducing the costs and delivery time that ATM owners had been experiencing. From there Jackson spent years diligently researching and gathering the specifications for products need by all makes and models of automatic teller machines. This critical information coupled with his enhanced production and distribution system allowed his company to successfully penetrate the national market. Systemax quickly gained national recognition for its ability to provide high quality ATM products, at greatly reduced cost in less than half the time as his competitors. Today the company has expanded its offering to include proprietary waste management solutions that drive national client's costs down even further.

The existing headquarters building is filled to capacity and plans for yet another expansion is on the drawing board. In the few years since it was founded, this small company has clearly put its mark on the world of automated banking. Systemax® brand ATM products and services are used around the world.

Springfield 143

chapter | **twelve**

12

HEALTH CARE & EDUCATION

University of Illinois at Springfield, 144-145
Doctors Hospital, 146
Lincoln Land Community College, 147
Robert Morris College, 148

Photo by Terry Farmer

University of Illinois at Springfield

UIS offers a beautifully maintained campus with lots of green spaces and study areas.

In 1970, on the eve of the opening of the university's first classes, Founding President Robert Spencer stood before his 45 charter faculty members and handful of working staff and spoke about the magnitude of what they were about to do. He reminded them of the enormous risk of inaugurating a new university and expressed hope that "their work would be of significance to the people of central Illinois for generations to come."

Three decades later, the University of Illinois at Springfield is fulfilling its promise to the region. The beautiful, 746-acre campus on the southern edge of Abraham Lincoln's hometown has become one of the Midwest's premier liberal arts institutions. It is regarded as an invaluable resource for area business as well as for Illinois' governmental hub. State and federal agencies and business associations rely on the expertise and research capabilities of UIS faculty and seek out skilled UIS graduates to recruit.

The citizens of Springfield and the surrounding communities have access to such campus treasures as Brookens Library, the three-time national championship Prairie Stars soccer team, and the 2000-seat Sangamon Auditorium with its exceptional array of cultural entertainment.

What President Spencer may not have predicted a generation ago was the overwhelming success of his vision of a university that emphasizes public affairs. UIS, through its ties to state government and commitment to public service, has made lessons of civic and global understanding, ethical behavior, and the great traditions of democracy an integral part of the curriculum. Learning flourishes as students of all ages are recognized as individuals. They interact with professors in small classes and have enviable access to practical internship experience. While they pursue diverse careers in business, education, criminal justice, social work, and a myriad of other fields, they graduate equally qualified for the challenges of a global economy.

UIS is committed to preparing students not only for lives of meaningful work, but also for lives of meaning. Innovative teaching methods and the latest technology are celebrated but take no higher priority than imparting the basic and transferable skills of inquiry, analysis, and communication. As a result, UIS graduates emerge with the capacity for lifelong learning and the ability to invent and reinvent themselves.

As one of three campuses of the world-class University of Illinois, UIS is increasingly earning a national reputation for excellence. Student enrollment exceeds 4,000 and is comprised of traditional residential students and full and part-time non-traditional students—those returning to school to finish a degree and working adults seeking advanced or second degrees or professional programs.

In the fall of 2001, UIS welcomed its first class of Capital Scholars, a small group of highly motivated, highly qualified first- and second-year students. The history-making enrollment of these lower division students marked the end of an era of serving only juniors, seniors, and graduate students. The Capital Scholars program brings a new energy and vitality to the campus and underscores the importance that UIS attaches to its public affairs mission, through a core curriculum emphasizing the mastery of scholarship and leadership skills.

Four colleges, Education and Human Services; Business and Management; Liberal Arts and Sciences; and Public Affairs and Administration, offer a total of 20 undergraduate and 18 master's degree programs. There is also a doctoral program in public administration.

Classrooms and laboratories at UIS offer the latest in computer technology, cable television, and other equipment.

Norris L. Brookens Library has a collection of more than 516,000 volumes and is linked via computer to 44 academic libraries in Illinois.

Members of the charter class of Capital Scholars relax in Lincoln Residence Hall.

UIS is a leader in online education, while also offering broadcast and interactive television courses. Distance learning is enabling UIS to increase it ability to serve the public by reaching place bound students. Excellence in instruction is reflected in part in the national recognition given UIS accounting majors who have one of the highest CPA exam pass rates in the nation. In addition, students completing the university's teaching sequence have had 100 percent pass rates on Illinois certification exams.

The Norris L Brookens Library, the finest academic research facility in the area, supports curriculum needs but is also a valuable resource to the general public. Beyond its own holdings of more than half a million volumes, the library provides a full range of materials through interlibrary loan collaboration with other libraries, the ILLINET Online system, specialized databases and the Internet.

Foreign exchange programs expand UIS' diversity as well as its global offerings. Students from more than 45 different countries attend classes at UIS. Study-abroad programs expose students further into the international realm.

One of the most exciting developments to take place recently has been the partnership forged with the new Abraham Lincoln Presidential Library and Museum. The alliance with one of the world's most distinguished libraries will bring the university national attention and support its ongoing Lincoln-related academic initiatives. The partnership will benefit UIS students through access to internationally known scholars and enhance resource on the 16th president and Civil War. And UIS' new Distinguished Chair in Lincoln Studies is held by one of the nation's foremost Lincoln scholars, Phillip J. Paludan.

Also bringing national attention to the university are the UIS Prairie Stars athletic teams. Teams in five competitive sports—men's and women's tennis, women's basketball, women's volleyball and men's soccer—have earned numerous honors and titles. The men's soccer team has brought home three national championship trophies under the leadership of legendary coach Aydin O. Gonulsen, who retired after the 2001 season.

Campus life builds camaraderie through a variety of pastimes such as music, plays, movies, clubs and organizations, and special day trips for activities such as skiing and canoeing.

More than 30 years after founding President Spencer addressed his fledgling campus community, UIS continues to fulfill his vision of a new university—one that serves its community and state and produces students that are not only highly employable but also highly educated.

The Public Affairs Center houses administrative offices, Sangamon Auditorium, Studio Theatre, the Food Emporium, bookstore, and the Conference Center.

Doctors Hospital

In the words of one patient who has used Doctors Hospital facilities several times "I've always been greeted by pleasant faces and it makes such a difference." Treating clients in a personalized manner is a goal Doctors Hospital has set for itself as a part of providing high quality healthcare services in a convenient, efficient manner.

Situated in a part of the Springfield metropolitan area that has seen a 62 percent growth since the 1990 census, Doctors Hospital has also expanded since being built in 1975. The four-story hospital located on the south side of Springfield is now on a campus that includes the Medical Office Plaza, a support services building, and a Professional Office Building (POB). The Plaza and the POB offer physicians office space. The POB also has an outpatient surgery suite with two operating rooms, an outpatient radiology suite with two x-ray rooms, a mamography suite, and three procedure rooms. A hospital emergency room (ER) with full access to imaging, laboratory, and cardiopulmonary services, is open 24-hours a-day. Doctors Hospital prides itself on its ability to have ER patients in the hands of a health provider within five minutes of arrival.

Doctors Hospital is a fully accredited, licensed, 177-bed acute care facility. Through Health Management Limited Partnership created in 1988, it is majority owned by 52 active Springfield area physicians. There are 84 doctors with active medical privileges as staff members. Among them are multiple medical specialties that allow for a multidisciplinary approach in meeting the healthcare needs of patients.

The hospital offers inpatient medical/surgical, intensive care, and psychiatric care. Surgical facilities are ready 24 hours a day to handle very complex to basic surgical procedures. An eight-bed intensive care unit offers up-to-date monitoring equipment as well as a caring medical team to closely provide for the critically ill. The psychiatric unit works with geriatric and the chronically mentally ill as well as those suffering from anxiety and depression.

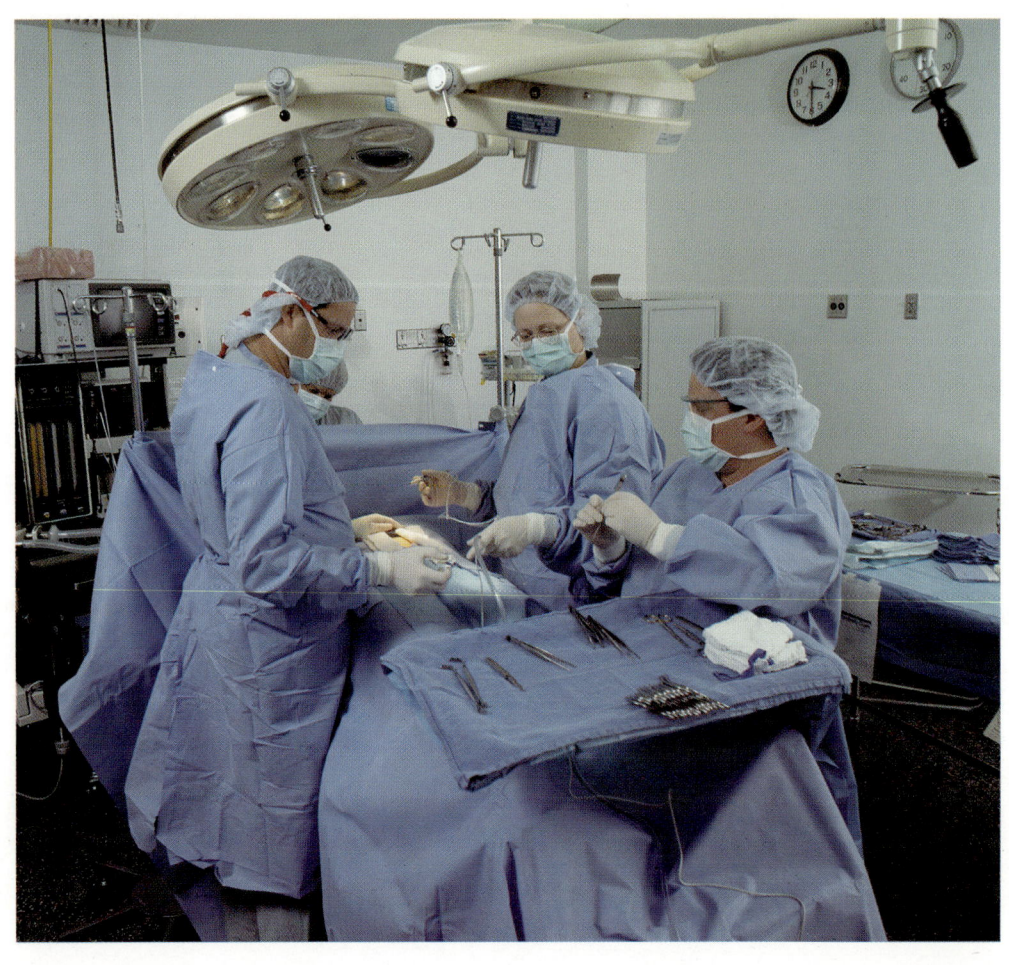

Outpatient services are innumerable. Whether it is diagnostic imaging, lab work by medical technologist and pathologists, cosmetic surgery, rehabilitation therapy, or orthopedic surgery, Doctors Hospital has a full spectrum of offerings.

Always planning for improvement Doctors Hospital has a number of projects under discussion and some ready for implementation. A Back Institute serving those with acute back pain and Corporate Health Solutions which provides businesses with services ranging from health screenings to managing worker compensation injury and illness cases are just two examples.

With Doctors Hospitals' recognition of the humanity of their clients as an integral part of healthcare, through upgrading of equipment, programs, staff training, and medical services, the Springfield community and associated rural areas will continue to benefit greatly from this important medical facility.

Lincoln Land Community College

Lincoln Land Community College (LLCC) has taken the "community" in its name to heart, serving students from a diverse range of ages, backgrounds, ethnicity, skills, interests, wants, and needs. Comprehensive transfer degree programs entice a large number of undergraduates attracted by quality, affordable, accessible education that enables them to begin curriculums leading to baccalaureate degrees. Graduation from LLCC means transferability to four-year colleges and universities. General associate degrees, as well as occupational and technical degrees and certificate programs, pave the way for successful entry into the workforce or for career advancement as employees. Personal enrichment non-credit classes and workshops give many the satisfaction and enjoyment that comes from learning useful skills or new hobbies.

Founded in 1967, LLCC opened in a temporary location and buildings the following year and moved to its permanent campus in 1974. Since then there has been great physical growth in buildings and facilities with state-of-the-art technology and design. While the main campus is located on the south side of Springfield, no student in its 4,115-square-mile-area is more than 25 miles from an LLCC facility. Telecourses and on-line courses are also an option. Community College District 526 is made up of all or parts of 15 counties and is the largest such district in Illinois. In addition to the main campus, there are six Regional Education Centers in the district and four specialized centers in Springfield.

Since the college is largely tax-supported, area residents elect seven members of the eight-member board of trustees with the eighth being a student elected from the campus. Tuition costs are kept at a minimum, making higher education readily available to greater numbers of students. Small class size, qualified faculty—whose main purpose is to teach rather than to do research or publish —along with special help provided by writing, math, study skills, and other centers practically guarantee student success. The centers are staffed by faculty and peer helpers.

Adult education programs help students earn their GEDs, learn English as a second language, acquire employability skills, and achieve occupational certifications. Senior citizens participate in activities, tours, and talks in LLCC's Academy of Lifelong Learning, covering every topic from architecture and gardening to local history and travel. Children in the Youth Enrichment Services' hands-on programs explore everything from signing to foreign languages, from pioneers to space travel. High school students get a head start on first year college classes or ACT preparation. Federal, state, and local government employees receive customized training on new equipment, procedures, and computer programs at the Capital City Center. In addition to its academic offerings, LLCC boasts numerous clubs and winning sports teams. Its students were the first in the world from a community college to enter a solar car in the Formula Sun Grand Prix. The many opportunities at Lincoln Land Community College support its mission to serve the community with diverse quality education.

The many opportunities at Lincoln Land Community College support its mission to serve the community with diverse quality education.

In addition to the main campus, there are six Regional Education Centers in the district and four specialized centers in Springfield.

Robert Morris College

The Robert Morris College Springfield Campus.

Since its founding in 1988, Robert Morris College has grown to become an established and contributing institution in the Springfield community, focused on educating and preparing students for the world of work in today's rapidly changing corporate environment. Course work and teaching methods are geared toward educating the whole student, ensuring that each student's college experience is relevant and stimulating. Robert Morris offers academic choices allowing students to opt for continuing their education, going to work, or both. RMC is the fastest growing private college in Illinois.

Originally chartered as a junior college in Carthage, Illinois in 1965, Robert Morris College is now a not-for-profit, baccalaureate degree-granting institution, accredited by the Commission on Institutions of Higher Education of the North Central Association of Colleges and Schools. The College acquired the Moser School of Business in Chicago and opened an RMC campus in the city's financial district in 1975. Relocated in 1998 to the Second Leiter Building, the main campus of Robert Morris College has become a viable addition to the educational and cultural corridor of Chicago's south loop.

In the late 1980s RMC began an aggressive expansion program throughout the state. The Carthage campus was moved to Springfield to better serve the needs of residents in central Illinois. Since establishing the Springfield campus, the College has consistently participated in civic, social, and community efforts, most recently sponsoring a workforce audit with the city of Springfield and the Chamber of Commerce.

The Chicago, Springfield, Orland Park, DuPage campuses, plus centers near O'Hare Airport, Peoria, and Joliet, together form the Robert Morris College network of service to students in Illinois. Today, RMC offers bachelor's degrees in computer studies, graphic design and business administration. Robert Morris College is also the state's leading provider of associate degrees to minority students.

The RMC commitment to higher education in Illinois is threefold: matching curricula to the changing needs of employers, nurturing the educational aspirations of all students, and ensuring relevance to life and work. Faculty and staff are committed to providing the structure and guidance geared to promoting student success. RMC students acquire real life working experience by participating in an internship directly related to his or her field of study. Students are also encouraged to participate in the school's rich offerings of sports and cultural events. RMC has an active varsity lineup and is currently adding to the athletic opportunities at its Springfield campus.

Real world education experience with a focused career foundation is why employers vie for RMC graduates. And not surprisingly, it is also why 91 percent of RMC students find jobs upon graduation. The Robert Morris College experience offers a unique educational opportunity in the Springfield area.

The Robert Morris College Athletics Program continues to grow in Springfield with the addition of more team sports for both men and women.

Photo by Terry Farmer

Springfield **151**

chapter | **thirteen**

13

REAL ESTATE, DEVELOPMENT & CONSTRUCTION

Siciliano, Inc., 152-155
FWAI Architects Inc., 156-157
Orchard Park Apartments, 158-159
R.D. Lawrence Construction Company, LTD., 160
Perry Broughton Trucking & Excavating, Inc., 161
Vancil Contracting Inc., 162
P.H. Broughton & Sons, Inc., 163

Photo by Terry Farmer

Siciliano, Inc.

Dana Thomas Residence Restoration–Hasbrouck–Peterson Architects.

With over 33 years of growth behind it, Siciliano Inc. has become a leader in the general construction contracting market in Springfield and central Illinois. From modest beginnings as a demolition/excavation contractor the company has expanded from project to project, striving to combine quality craftsmanship with innovative ideas while completing the job on time and under budget. Each day and every new job bring challenges and learning opportunities that give Siciliano the skills and knowledge to create, restore, and rebuild to the highest standards. The company has earned its reputation as a premier provider of construction services by satisfying a diverse range of clients from the State of Illinois Capital Development Board to a private hotel developer. Siciliano's dedication to quality and customer satisfaction gained it a listing in *Inc.* magazine in 1991 and 1992, making it, at that time, the only Springfield company to ever appear twice. A number of high profile projects such as restoration of the Dana-Thomas House, construction of the Crowne Plaza Hotel, renovation of the Old State Capitol Plaza, and building of the world-renowned Abraham Lincoln Presidential Library have made the company's red, green, and white sign a familiar sight in Springfield. Siciliano offers commercial and industrial construction, historical restoration, underground utilities work, site development, and demolition among other services.

Frank Siciliano founded the company in 1968 performing demolition and excavation work. Siciliano gradually expanded services to include backfilling, compacting, and grading. With the arrival of Rick Lawrence in 1989 the company moved into general construction. Lawrence brought to the firm a strong background in the construction industry including crucial skills in bidding and managing a variety of projects. With this knowledge, Lawrence led Siciliano into bidding for State of Illinois construction projects. Their first successful bid was a remodeling job at the Illinois State Fairgrounds. This initial State of Illinois project allowed the firm to get its feet wet in the world of government contracts and begin to gain the experience and knowledge necessary to become a successful bidder on other public projects.

But Lawrence also recognized a market that was not being served—public and private organizations seeking a single company, with expertise in everything from demolition, site preparation, and construction and world-class-quality preservation artisanship to complete a single job. Lawrence set about to create that company out of

New Salem Visitors Center–Metzger Johnson Architects, Inc.

Siciliano, once known primarily for its demolition and excavation services. Siciliano's first major job as a general contractor, and one that put it on the local map for creativity and dynamism was the restoration of the Dana-Thomas House in Springfield. Renowned architect Frank Lloyd Wright designed the historic Dana-Thomas House, built in 1903. The State of Illinois, which purchased the house in 1981, spent three years and $5 million to restore the structure to its prime. Recognized as "the most complete, best preserved, and most elaborate of Frank Lloyd Wright's early 'Prairie Houses', it is toured by thousands of visitors annually." Siciliano acted as general contractor on the final historic restoration phase of the project. Just as Frank Lloyd Wright, as a rising young architect, was given an opportunity to experiment with new design ideas and technologies, Siciliano crews set about to refine plastering and other skills to a high degree of perfection. The artisanship needed was at a level far beyond that required in general construction. The words of Susan Lawrence Dana, the woman who commissioned the house, upon its completion are equally appropriate for the restoration work of Siciliano construction today: "It would not have been possible for careless, or incompetent, or indifferent artisans to have brought about the results obtained in this building." For its work on the Dana-Thomas House, Siciliano received the prestigious Madigan Award from the Capital Development Board.

From this, one of the most visible tourist sites in the city, Siciliano crews moved underground to handle "the most unique sewer repair project in the city's history." Springfield's Old Town Branch was an open waterway that was covered over to form a storm water sewer beginning in the 1850s. Though unseen by most residents, it is a vital part of the city's infrastructure. Using a unique boring and pipe jacking operation performed 25 feet below grade, Siciliano crews placed 148 sections of pipe, each measuring 7 1/2 feet long, 14 feet in diameter, and weighing 23 tons.

New Salem, Illinois is host to over a half million visitors annually who come to experience life in a recreated pioneer village of the 1830s when it was home to young

New Abraham Lincoln Presidential Library— Hellmuth, Obata & Kassabaum, Inc.

UIS-Lincoln Hall—Solomon Cordwell Buenz and Associates, Inc.

Abraham Lincoln. The site had long been lacking in an appropriate welcoming center to orient tourists, provide an auditorium, and host changing exhibits. A $2 million Visitors Center was proposed in 1990 and Siciliano was the successful bidder. This spacious center has a large seating capacity auditorium with raised roof and gallery area featuring exposed wood framing. An inviting reception/entry space, and workshop areas complete this multi-use facility. Though massive in scale, it was built to camouflage its great size and not overwhelm the historic village. Siciliano also constructed the state-owned, privately managed New Salem restaurant with its rustic exposed wood framing and large semi-circle dining area.

By this time Siciliano had proved its mettle in both fast track and high quality work and was ready for a new challenge. The Raynor Corporation was developing the city's largest and most luxurious hotel named, appropriately, the Crowne Plaza. Siciliano won the bid for the foundations and poured concrete structure work. The job again brought out Lawrence and his staff's creativity and can-do commitment to the table. "Heavily reinforced concrete floor slabs, supported by exceptionally large concrete columns, are rising at a rate of one every two weeks" marveled *Construction Digest* magazine in a feature cover story during hotel construction. The one-of-a-kind nature of the construction was evident from the start. With 17,000 square feet per floor, the building was designed and built to withstand any possible earthquake, a real threat in the region. Variety of floor heights from 22 feet down to 10 feet as well as its proportions (exceptionally narrow for its height) required incredible strengthening of support elements. The high quality of work and commitment to schedule allowed Siciliano to negotiate with the developer for the $12 million interior finish and $3.5 million west tower phases. Siciliano and Raynor gave Springfield a premier luxury hotel and convention facility. At the conclusion of this project in June 1997, Siciliano, Inc. was purchased by Rick Lawrence.

With the successful completion of this materials-dense project, Siciliano was the natural choice to bid on and win the contract to repair a major parking garage centered in the State of Illinois' Capitol Complex that experienced structural failure. The job again merited a Construction Digest cover story, which called Siciliano's innovative solution "expedient and cost effective." Precast double T-beams had developed failures and cracking, endangering the structure. Siciliano employed a unique system of injecting epoxy behind steel plates laminated on each beam. "Siciliano," noted the article, "has been involved with some of central Illinois' most high profile projects" and "is widely known for bringing jobs in on time, every time."

Other recently completed projects in the Springfield area include restoration work at the Statehouse, renovation of the Old State Capitol Plaza, construction of Lincoln Hall, the new freshmen residence hall at the

Crowne Plaza Hotel & Convention Center—FWAI Architects, Inc.

University of Illinois at Springfield, and grandstand facility of the new rodeo arena at the Illinois State Fairgrounds.

Siciliano's high profile commitments to quality work, timely completion, and client satisfaction are currently exhibited at possibly the most significant building in Springfield, one that will become known throughout the world—the Abraham Lincoln Presidential Library and Museum. Designed by famed architect Gyo Obata, the 230,000-square-foot complex, costing over $155 million will dominate the central city. This world-class library and museum will be the single-most important destination for scholars and the general public to learn about Abraham Lincoln, an internationally revered figure. Siciliano has the general work contract to construct the library phase of the project which consists of a 100,000 square-foot structure estimated to cost about $25 million.

The quality caliber of the Siciliano employees is another factor in the company's success. As one of the larger union employers in the area, Siciliano has 12 craft unions represented on its work force. The individuals who make up the Siciliano team have a passion for the work of construction. Coming to the firm with varying degrees of expertise, this dedicated staff uses their daily experiences to improve their knowledge and skills. Without the dedication, commitment, and care of its talented employees, Siciliano would never have become a leading presence in central Illinois construction.

Siciliano employees give back to the community in which they live. The company actively participates in fund-raising activities for the Hope School for Special Needs Children and St. Joseph's retirement home and

Vachel Lindsay Residence Restoration—Gilmore Franzen Architects, Inc.

provides no-charge services to several local non-profit agencies. Siciliano sponsors bowling and softball teams. Students seeking careers in the construction industry can apply for a Siciliano-funded scholarship through the National AGC Education and Research Foundation. In these and other ways, Siciliano demonstrates commitment to quality of life and social services in Springfield.

From its origins in demolition and excavation work Siciliano has become a major force in building a new Springfield and restoring the best from the past. The company has earned a reputation for handling tight schedules with its can do approach to solving tough construction issues by seeking innovative ways to complete them. An entrepreneurial spirit pervades the company and a synergy among Siciliano employees assures continued expansion of operations and an ever-increasing reputation for the highest quality, detail, and craftsmanship in every project large or small.

New Rodeo Arena Grandstand—Ferry & Associates Architects, Inc.

FWAI Architects Inc.

Broadwell Building (corporate offices).

In 1976 when Carl Fischer and his wife, Kay, established Carl Fischer Associates, the office was in their home. With drawing board, rulers, pens, and paper, Carl set to work designing buildings for both the private and public sector while Kay took on the role of office manager/secretary/treasurer. Their combined efforts gave the firm the good footings and philosophies that make them successful today. August Wisnosky, a high school classmate of Carl's, joined the firm in 1982, bringing a special interest in historic restoration, construction document procedures, and project budget estimating to the firm's growing areas of expertise. Now known as FWAI Architects, the firm has a fourth principal in architect Paul Wheeler and employees that share in ownership through an Employee Stock Option Plan.

With a staff of 20, which includes registered architects, architectural technicians, administrative staff, interior designers, and a field observer, there is a strong team approach to project solutions. The client is also an integral part of the team. The firm, with its planning, architectural design, interior design, and construction services, has a well-deserved reputation of excellence not only among the clients served, but from the architectural community as well. The American Institute of Architects has awarded the firm several design awards. From as far away as Finland and in states as large as Texas, the FWAI name can be found associated with new buildings, additions, the remodeling of structures, and historic restoration.

Whatever the need, service is the focus. A key component in providing the excellence in service that sets the firm apart from others, is its communication systems. Through in-house e-mail and a mail routing system, each member of the team working on a project is kept up-to-date on all developments. The project manager is well informed about the contacts maintained with the client.

Crowne Plaza Hotel.

These systems extend beyond the FWAI offices to networking with a pool of experts across the country. A "File Transfer Protocol" (FTP) site is one such system. FWAI architects can share their design drawings with consultants in other states and the consultants can exchange their drawings with the architects by "posting" them on-line. All graphic design work and presentations are created in-house, often with the aid of software that allows the client three-dimensional virtual tours and flexibility in seeing color and texture options for their proposed facility.

To keep their ideas fresh, a diverse range of projects from small to very large is a part of FWAI's portfolio. To their credit is the planning and interior design of a design award winning 500-square-foot jewelry store interior to the planning and design of a 480,000-square-foot hotel and conference center. FWAI also prides themselves with having completed projects that have specialized requirements. The Sangamon County Juvenile Detention Center Design/Build Project involved safety, security, material durability, and space control above the ordinary. "FWAI's project management was thorough and directed specifically to the specifications required" was the complimentary response from the county. As a design/build project, FWAI was involved with the project from concept to completion, including site selection evaluations.

A national insurance firm, Blue Cross Blue Shield, is one of FWAI's returning clients, often making use of existing structures and contracting with FWAI for space planning services. They depend on FWAI to turn current spaces into economically functional facilities where the workflow patterns, furniture, and equipment selections create an efficient and comfortable workplace.

Planning, whether for a remodeling or a new structure, involves site visits and interviews with the staff that will use the facility. The conversion of Kennedy Hall at McFarland Mental Health Center for housing and schooling of forensic adolescents is an example FWAI uses to point out the value they see in site visits and interviews with personnel. Those who work on a day-by-day basis with the youths provided a perspective that might not otherwise have been recognized as design issues had FWAI not involved themselves in this step.

Historic restoration adds another dimension to the challenges accepted. Among projects in Springfield, FWAI has completed the restoration work on the State Fairgrounds

Sangamon County Complex.

Main Gate, the Lincoln Tomb, the houses in the Lincoln Home National Historic Site, and the Dana-Thomas House. The Illinois Historic Preservation Agency expressed their satisfaction with FWAI's "attention to detail and their sensitivity." FWAI's own offices in the 1917 Broadwell Drugstore Building speak of their respect for historic architecture.

New architectural design is the primary service of FWAI and one in which they excel. Whether it is the sleek contemporary look of the firehouse for the Air National Guard, the traditional design of the Sangamon County Complex that fits in with the historic structures in nearby downtown, the Prairie Style of a bank, or the English Tudor-Revival look of condominiums, as architects, the FWAI staff sets an aesthetic and contextually pleasing design as a priority, as well as functionality and economic feasibility.

With procedures that involve teamwork, respect for all ideas put forth, full utilization of talented staff, and active communication between staff and client, FWAI has a formula that has proven successful time and time again.

Ronald Reagan Boyhood Home.

Orchard Park Apartments

It is with a passion that Dr. Fred Fleury absorbs himself in each subject that catches his interest. It was real estate and energy-efficiency at the same time, when he purchased his first rental property, a duplex in 1981. After taking an energy-conservation course at Sangamon State University (now UIS), the gynecologist set about putting into practice what he had learned. Rehabilitating older utility systems, though, proved to be more costly than new construction so, on land purchased in 1982, he designed and developed his first super-insulated and passive solar apartment complex. Now known as Orchard Park North, it is located in the 300 block of North Park and 1200 block of Orchard Avenue. This project won him the U.S. Department of Energy's 1985 National Awards Program for Energy Innovation. It was one of only twenty-seven to be so awarded in the United States that year.

Fleury continued to design and develop three other complexes—the Jefferson Street Apartments at 1208 & 1212 west; Orchard Park South on South 4th Street and Orchard Park Seven Pines on Seven Pines Road where the main offices are located. Foot thick double walls and 20 inches of attic insulation combined with high-efficiency heat pumps and passive solar water heaters in all electric buildings have proven their worth for these complexes in low utility bills year after year.

Orchard Park Apartments, under Fleury Enterprises Incorporated, now operate 854 apartments in eight Springfield locations with Dr. Fleury and his wife, Barbara as president and vice-president. Barbara Fleury who at one time, managed both her husband's medical practice office and the apartments, has also been very involved with Orchard Park. Renters may choose from one to three bedroom apartments that vary in price and amenities depending upon location and size. Their appeal attracts professionals to college students. Three of the facilities Dr. Fleury built have swimming pools; all have on-site laundry rooms or individual washer and dryer hook-ups, garbage disposals, dishwashers, and ceiling fans.

Significant changes in the rental market in recent years have increased the demand for corporate apartments, so called because initially, their main use was for personnel corporations assigned to local offices on an as-needed basis. In five years Orchard Park Apartments went from 20 to 50 of these furnished suites available for short-term leases. Corporations are not the only ones using the apartments. Businesses and medical facilities employee more and more contract employees—technicians, consultants, analysts—who are in Springfield for only a short time. Corporate apartments are a more cost-effective option than hotels and motels for housing the employees and are comfortable and convenient. As this

Photo by Terry Farmer

trend continues Orchard Park expects to convert more apartments to corporate use.

As a privately owned and operated business, Orchard Park has great flexibility with the suites, providing one-month, 6-month, or year leases. On occasion even weekly rates are offered. Because of this, Orchard Park serves a number of customers outside the traditional corporate world. A short term lease is especially helpful to people whose homes sell before they are ready to move into their new place; to those who have been transferred to the Springfield area but haven't yet found a place to buy; families that may have suffered a home disaster such as a fire; and visiting relatives for whom there is not enough space in the home. There are also tenants who simply enjoy having a furnished apartment—one such tenant, for example, has been in an Orchard Park suite over 5 years.

The Orchard Park Suites are homes away from home. They come with everything from a colander in which to drain spaghetti to a nightstand and alarm clock. Bed linens, towels, cable TV, free local telephone calls, and a management staff willing to help fill individual requests combine to make repeat business referrals frequent. A patio or deck adds to the pleasure of an Orchard Park suite. Each rental is furnished with hand-selected furniture and accessories so that no two are identical. Barbara Fleury has a knack for flower arranging and will often personally place silk flower arrangement in the rooms. Many of the accessories are items the Fleurys have purchased while traveling. The Orchard Park office manager remarks that you never know what might be in the boxes that arrive while the Fleurys are on vacation. Often they find attractive furniture, dishes, pots and pans and other items they pick up for the apartments. While semi-retired from apartment operations, the Fleurys' interest in them has not waned. It is not uncommon to find Dr. Fleury, himself showing an apartment during an open house, for example.

For all of the Orchard Park apartment complexes, preventative maintenance practices are firmly adhered to. A three-page checklist is used before any new renter moves in. There are constant up-dates in carpeting and appliances and walls are routinely painted to keep apartments fresh and desirable places to call home. A staff member can be reached 24 hours a day for any emergencies and regularly make themselves available for weekend move-ins. "We have maintenance, cleaning, and administrative staff that work like family. Some of them have been with us for 14 years or more, " said the manager. There certainly is pride expressed in the facilities and services that Orchard Park Apartments are able to offer to tenants—a unique living experience in Springfield.

Photo by Terry Farmer

R.D. Lawrence Construction Company, LTD.

One hundred eighty feet up in the dome of the Capitol Building or 45 feet down in the earth at the Lake Springfield water treatment plant, R.D. Lawrence Construction Company has shown it has the experience in meeting a variety of construction challenges.

John Goetz, an engineer by education, is the owner of the firm that began with Richard D. Lawrence in 1959. Working within a 50-mile radius of Springfield, Goetz has led his company in numerous building projects in the commercial, industrial, and institutional realms—schools, hospitals, factories, and department stores. Restoration projects also have a place in the diversity of work the general contracting firm has undertaken. In each instance Goetz has placed emphasis on staying within budget, keeping on schedule, and above all, quality. Bringing to timely completion a quality project, is a key characteristic in the reputation John Goetz expects of his company.

The increasingly popular Design/Build program, where the client has just one entity to control all aspects of a building project is one in which the company takes special pride. The Farmers State Bank and Trust in Jacksonville is an example where Goetz's company managed the project from the idea stage through completion—arranging for the architect and specialist needed, estimating cost, setting time lines, taking bids, and seeing the project through to it timely completion. An extensive database of experts—engineers to suppliers—as well as the access to equipment and craftsmen needed, has been developed through their years of experience.

R.D. Lawrence Construction has equipment and employees for concrete, structural steel erection, carpentry, and millwright work. They are one of the few companies in the area with millwright capabilities and the equipment and experience to meet the demands of this construction user.

Among accomplishments, R. D. Lawrence Construction looks to is the number of repeat customers: 25 years of work for Passavant Area Hospital in Jacksonville, and 20 years of successful projects at Nestle Beverage Co. and National Starch & Chemical Co. to name a few. The challenging installation of the Claricone system that doubled the water purification capacity of a clarifier at Lake Springfield, the restoration work at the State Capitol Building and other notable historic sites attests to the abilities of R.D. Lawrence. The company has successfully completed several phases of the State Capitol restoration. The project that caught the most attention was the exceptional transformation of the interior dome from dark with soot and grime to a bright, colorful jewel. The project won for R.D. Lawrence Construction Company a Special Award for Restoration from the American Institute of Architects (AIA). Part of the work required the hand assembly of an amazing 150 tons of scaffolding used to enable workers to reach a height of some 200 feet.

John Goetz is a past-president and an active member of the Central Illinois Builders of AGC (Associated General Contractor's of America). He embraces the attributes of skill, integrity, and responsibility that the association promotes. It is with this attitude of professionalism that R.D. Lawrence Construction Company and its employees operate on each project they undertake.

Farmers State Bank & Trust, Jacksonville, Illinois.

Interior Dome Restoration, Illinois State Capitol Building, Springfield. Photo by Terry Farmer

Perry Broughton Trucking & Excavating, Inc.

When Perry Broughton Trucking & Excavating, Inc. was working the sites for the Clock Tower commercial development and the old Fiat Allis plant, these areas were considered the far west and south sides of Springfield. Land developments now extend miles further. Just as Springfield has grown in the past 30 years so has the business that husband and wife, Perry and Rachel Broughton, founded in 1972. At that time they had but one end loader, a tandem, a tractor-trailer, and a lowboy. The equipment inventory today includes bulldozers, excavators, backhoes, trenchers, pavers, rollers, trucks, a concrete curb machine, and a crane. Within a few years of the business' beginnings, Perry's brother John became an integral part of the company and now serves as one of its officers.

In the business' early years, the equipment was based in Pawnee at the Broughtons' farm, but as the business grew and the need for a Springfield location became apparent, a commercial building was constructed in 1979 at 1227 West Enos Avenue. Continued growth resulted in the purchase of additional adjoining land. By 1995, the office building was expanded providing more shop and office space. The Enos location remains as its headquarters.

Perry Broughton Trucking and Excavating's primary customers are in commercial and government sectors. Whether it is site preparation for a new hotel, expansion around a hospital, or construction of a highway, Broughtons provide complete services from earth excavation to asphalt and concrete flatwork. They have the expertise in grading, installing water mains, sanitary and storm sewers, box culverts, curbs and gutters, asphalt, and concrete paving.

The demand in the construction business is known for its highs and lows but through them all, Broughtons take pride in the quality of their work while keeping prices competitive. In 1996 the Illinois Department of Transportation recognized Perry Broughton Trucking & Excavating as the recipient of the state's Award of Excellence for a Small Construction Project. The Award of Excellence was presented for quality workmanship which, in this case, was completed before the contracted time schedule. The project included the removal of a railroad overpass and reconstruction of the pavement that served a number of businesses. Economically, the businesses lost revenue every day the road was closed; therefore time was of the essence and Perry Broughton Trucking & Excavating more than met the challenge.

The Springfield community and surrounding area has been enriched by Perry Broughton Trucking & Excavating's quality work and also by their sense of civic and social responsibility. They support a variety of charitable organizations and youth programs with 4-H and Boy Scouts being special favorites.

Establishing and maintaining a family business is a difficult task that Perry, Rachel, and John Broughton and their employees have met with goal setting, determination, hard work, and integrity. They have accomplished much as they build roads and developments. However, their greatest construction project has been the building of a remarkable business.

Rachel, Perry, and John Broughton, officers of Perry Broughton Trucking & Excavating, Inc, 1227 West Enos Avenue, Springfield. Photo by Terry Farmer

Vancil Contracting Inc.

Vancil Contracting in its present form was founded in 1996. Its roots in the community, however, extend much deeper. Owner Ron Vancil has nearly 40 years experience in the local construction trade and has been involved with some of Springfield's most recognizable buildings — Nelson Center in Lincoln Park, Lincoln Library, Phase One of Lincoln Land Community College, Lincoln Home Visitors Center, and the Dallman I, II, and III power plant at Lake Springfield. The work of firms like Vancil Contracting is literally changing the face of Springfield. From $200,000 in projects in 1996, its first year in business, Vancil Contracting quickly gained a presence in the Springfield market, completing over $7,000,000 in project work in 2000, the first year of a new century of growth.

The success and growth of VanCon, as the firm is often known, is based on several factors including a focus on demanding and difficult projects. Other factors are the ability to sit down with clients and conceptualize estimates while developing a workable budget. Vancil maintains a balance of projects in the areas of industrial, governmental, commercial, and pre-engineered. Two large-scale recently completed projects include construction of the middle school buildings in Pleasant Plains and Rochester, Illinois.

VanCon also has experience in historic preservation work ranging from façade renovation on buildings in downtown Lincoln, Illinois to the internationally known Frank Lloyd Wright-designed Dana Thomas House in Springfield. Also, restoration of the stunning Great Room of the former Illinois State Journal newspaper building on South Sixth Street in downtown Springfield should be noted. The building houses offices of the Illinois Historic Preservation Agency and is a showcase for preservation work.

Pre-engineered structures are increasingly becoming a standard in new construction. Among pre-engineered structures built by Vancil are Nudo Products Large Panel Building and the present facilities for Security Door and Hardware in Springfield.

It is not variety of building types alone that has gained Vancil satisfied clients but also its willingness to accommodate special needs. The Bob Evans restaurant in Springfield's Prairie Crossing development was completed in an astounding three months. Built in winter, employees erected a large tent over the rising building and worked literally day and night to finish the project.

Vancon's core group of diverse employees expands as the company grows. The dedication of these responsible and talented staff is a major reason for the company's success. Another is Vancil's willingness to adopt the latest technology. "We are very modern in software management programs" for example, comments company president Ron Vancil. Vancil Contracting is a firm that challenges its employees and offers them a stimulated work environment in which people can grow and thrive professionally. In turn these employees have made Vancil a recognizable force in the Springfield building industry.

120 days from groundbreaking. Photo by Terry Farmer

New Rochester Middle School. Photo by Terry Farmer

P.H. Broughton & Sons, Inc.

Descendents of founder P.H. Broughton: (left to right) great-grandson Joshua Broughton, grandsons Perry, John, and David Broughton. Photo by Terry Farmer

The Broughton name has long been prominent in Springfield for excavation and paving. After working for other contractors building railroad grades, roads, and hauling, in 1921 Perry H. Broughton established his own company. Broughton used horses, bottom dump wagons, and slips for hauling, constructing railroad embankments, and highways. He also hauled coal and dug basements for houses and commercial buildings. Broughton, who began using trucks in the mid-1920s, sold his last team of horses in 1932. Houses going up around the new Lake Springfield in the 1930s provided the firm with plenty of foundation work. Leora Broughton partnered with her husband, managing the company's books. The Broughtons had three sons. The two older began working in their early teens, driving trucks and making coal and rock deliveries. Their contribution was reflected by the company's name change to P.H. Broughton & Sons. With our nation at war, Bill and Bob began serving their country in World War II in 1941. In 1946, with the help of their GI Bill, the company added two airborne bulldozers, new trucks, a front shovel, and crawler endloader. They built basements, supplied, and hauled rock and shale for new roads at Capital Airport and numerous subdivisions.

The firm, which had been located behind the family home on Cleveland Avenue since 1933, moved to its own facility on Dorlan Avenue in 1951, then in 1956, to its present location on North Lincoln Avenue. The company expanded their business with the addition of oil trucks, chip spreaders, and a cold mix asphalt plant. In 1957 the company's main focus changed with the addition of a hot mix plant and portable plant enabling them to expand their paving operation to a 80-mile radius around Springfield.

In 1964 P.H. Broughton passed away. His wife Leora, who had always been an integral part of the business, and her sons continued expanding the operation with the addition of a ready mix plant and a sand and gravel pit. By 1973, it seemed prudent to separate the businesses so Leora and Bill retained ownership of P.H. Broughton & Sons, Inc. with Bill handling the duties of chief operating officer. Bob took ownership of the ready mix operation and Donald assumed ownership of Sangamon Valley Sand and Gravel. But close family affiliations continued across company lines with Bob and Donald remaining associated with the paving department of P.H. Broughton & Sons. At this time, Bill's son, David, joined the company, overseeing the daily operation of the asphalt plant and dispatching trucks. In 1991 Donald left P.H. Broughton & Sons to devote his attention full time to Sangamon Valley Sand and Gravel. Bob Broughton died in 1994, Bill in September 1999 and Leora in October 1999. Bill's sons, Perry and John, have been active in the construction business in the Springfield area doing earth excavation, heavy highway, and site work. With the passing of their father, they added their expertise in management and field skills with their brother David to run P.H. Broughton & Sons, bringing this 80-year-old company into the 21st Century.

Through the years, many grandchildren and other family members have worked at the company in diverse roles. In the spring of 2001, Perry and Leora's great-grandson, Joshua, joined the company thereby continuing the P.H. Broughton legacy.

Springfield 165

chapter fourteen

14

THE MARKETPLACE, HOSPITALITY & TOURISM

Renaissance Hotel, 166-167
Springfield Convention and Visitors Bureau, 168
White Oaks Mall, 169

Photo by Terry Farmer

Renaissance Hotel

Renaissance Springfield Hotel.

With just two weeks to prepare a surprise dinner party for 350 guests, a 5,000 balloon drop from the ballroom ceiling, elaborate theme decorations, audio-video equipment set-ups, and a special phone hook-up with the President of the United States, Renaissance Hotel staff were challenged to say the least. That challenge was met with total success and the guests and guest of honor had nothing but compliments on the evening. The event, a party for out-going Governor Jim Edgar, initiated by his wife, Brenda, and personal aides was only one of the countless entertainments the Renaissance hosts annually. Video messages were sent from former President Gerald Ford and Senator Bob Dole. The conversation, with then President George Bush Senior, went without a hitch.

Large events are not out of the ordinary for the Renaissance Hotel. Handling even entire conventions is fairly routine. The Grand Ballroom illuminated with chandeliers replicating those of the Governor's Mansion provides entertainment or meeting space for 720. Whether it's a group of 10 or several hundred the Renaissance has the meeting rooms, A-V equipment, and the food service needed. Strategically located next door to the Prairie Capital Convention Center, with its 40,000 square feet of main floor exhibit space, the 15 meeting rooms (depending upon room configurations) in the hotel can be supplemented with another 14 in the convention center. An attached underground walkway connects the two buildings. Breakfast, brunch, lunch, snacks, hors d'oeuvres, and dinner—whatever is required by a group—can be served both in the hotel and in the convention center. The Renaissance's chef oversees meals that are culinary pleasures, all attractively presented.

Dining at the Renaissance is a treat for not only guests of the hotel but the Springfield community. The Lindsay's Gallery Restaurant features a full range of choices, including heart healthy offerings, on its breakfast, lunch, and dinner menus. Sunday brunch is a favorite of locals, especially the Easter and Mother's Day brunch buffets. The restaurant takes its name from the reproductions of the artwork on its walls by nationally known Springfield poet and artist Vachel Lindsay.

A luxurious experience awaits the business traveler, conventioneer, or vacationer at the Renaissance. Located in historic downtown Springfield, the twelve-story building recalls traditional city architecture in its use of red brick. Rich dark cherry wood paneling, imported marble floors, and a lobby filled with antique furnishings create a subdued elegant atmosphere. Victorian antiques, many of them personally chosen by developer Bill Cellini and his wife, Julie, can be found throughout the hotel. While on a trip to Italy, they purchased a Murano glass chandelier that hangs today in the Floreale Room, a private banquet room. Bill and Julie were responsible for many of the dramatic and extraordinary touches in the hotel, which opened in 1985.

The Ottawa and Freeport rooms (Lincoln/Douglas Debate Sites) or the Governors Altgeld, Bond, Horner, and Yates hospitality suites remind guests of the importance of history in Illinois and in the state capital, Springfield. The exciting new Abraham Lincoln Presidential Library, a draw for national and international visitors, is just one block away. It is only a short walk to the Lincoln/Herndon Law Offices, the Old State Capital, the depot where Lincoln left Springfield to become a U.S. President, and to the only home Lincoln ever owned. The hotel's concierge can make arrangements for visiting other Springfield historic sites and places of

interest, as well. State, federal, and many other offices are located in the downtown central area close by the Renaissance.

Guests in the Renaissance's 316 sleeping rooms are provided with services that meet every away-from-home need and comfort. The rooms have complimentary cable TV, movie and video games, courtesy in-room coffee, tea, irons, ironing boards, hair dryers, and toiletries. Service and amenities are reminiscent of the era of big-city first-class hostelries. The top two floors of the Renaissance are private-key access, offering larger rooms, free standing full-length mirrors, marble topped coffee tables and the feel of a luxurious private home. Guests there have access to the Club Lounge with its beautiful view of the city, where a continental breakfast, and evening hors d'oeuvres and discounted cordials are served. Also on the top floors are the Presidential and Governor's Suites, which presidents have used and where governors have slept. The suites have living rooms and dining rooms furnished with high style antiques, and include a kitchen, wet bars, sunken tubs, and king-size four poster beds.

The Concourse Level houses the hotel's large swimming pool, for a relaxing swim after a long day. Some guests prefer to unwind with a workout in the health club where a full range of physical fitness equipment is available and then enjoy the soothing effects of the whirlpool or the redwood sauna.

Shuttle service to and from the Amtrak Station or Capital Airport is provided. Valet or self-service parking in the adjacent parking garage eases arrivals and departures. A warm welcome and courteous service is a hallmark of Renaissance life. And, this service makes each visit there special. The key to this service is an outstanding experienced professional staff of 200-plus. From the waiter in the Globe Tavern (named for the hotel where Abraham and Mary Lincoln lived their first year of marriage) or the attendant that takes care of each and every guest room, it is the staff that make every stay at the Renaissance a memorable experience.

Renaissance Ballroom.

Renaissance Conference Room.

Springfield Convention and Visitors Bureau

Tourism, an industry that brings in over $275 million annually to the Springfield economy, is big business locally. The Springfield Convention and Visitors Bureau shapes, promotes, and expands that industry, the hosting of visitors to Springfield. Over 5,000 in-coming phone calls per month (not to mention the mail and e-mail) indicate the interest that the Bureau has stimulated in the capital city. Staff provide information to the leisure traveler, schedule large school groups into major tourist sites, are a liaison for convention planners, and make meeting arrangements for international professionals.

With accommodations of over 4,000 sleeping rooms, 210,000 square feet of indoor meeting space, and outdoor facilities, visitors to the nationally known historic sites, state Capitol buildings, fine restaurants, shopping, and major events such as Air Rendezvous and the Illinois State Fair, parks, museums, and much, much more, receive valuable assistance from the Visitors Bureau.

When it comes to value, the free services of the Bureau can't be beat. Developing brochures, booklets, event calendars, and a fun Web-site are just the beginning of marketing Springfield as a destination. Staff members meet with photojournalists, guidebook authors, do direct mailings, attend trade shows, and contact organizations to get the word out. Local members of national organizations or meeting planners from outside the area find ready assistance with most aspects of convention or meeting planning, large or small. The staff coordinate hotel/motel arrangements, food services, media, parking, and transportation. They help with registration, information packets, are a resource for speakers, entertainers, spouse activities and tours. They even assist with follow-up tracking.

Each year the Bureau promotes hundreds of sites and events to visitors from all over the world.

Springfield is home to well over 30 luxury and economy hotel properties.

Since the late 1960s the Visitors' Bureau has been a part of Springfield's city government. Over the years not only have things such as the two-page typed listing of "what to see and do" changed to a 60 page magazine, but the focus of the Bureau now includes product development as well as marketing and visitor services. Two recent examples are the "Route 66" and "Looking for Lincoln" heritage tourism projects. Alliances with other towns and sites along Route 66 and locations with connections to Abraham Lincoln were made to plan tours, activities, and promotional materials. The "Route 66" project has drawn great international as well as U.S. interest from nostalgia buffs. The "Looking for Lincoln" project alerts visitors to numerous central Illinois spots (many often overlooked) that put Lincoln and his era in perspective.

As a destination marketing and management agency the Springfield Convention and Visitors Bureau has made Springfield the leading downstate Illinois tourism site. Whether it is finding ways to keep a few visiting relatives entertained or arranging for a major convention, courtesy, expertise, and service are readily available at the Bureau.

White Oaks Mall

The food court serves as a gathering spot for White Oaks Mall visitors. Photo by Randy Squires

White Oaks Mall, the largest enclosed shopping center between Chicago and St. Louis, has become a central Illinois institution in the quarter century since it opened. On opening day in August 1977, shoppers perceived the super-regional center being on the distant outskirts of Springfield. The new mall proved a stimulus for the city's phenomenal southwest retail growth. White Oaks Mall draws visitors from throughout central Illinois and is the centerpiece of Springfield's southwestern retail hub—the largest in the region. Developed by shopping center industry leader Melvin Simon and Associates in partnership with the Barker family, White Oaks offers a big city shopping experience. Anchored by Bergner's, Famous-Barr, and Sears, there are more than 115 specialty store offerings including industry leaders Abercrombie & Fitch, White Barn Candle Co., Victoria's Secret, American Eagle Outfitters, GAP, and Yankee Candle Company. White Oaks' market success has brought many proto-type stores, like C.J. Banks, abercrombie children's wear, and Hollister Co. to Springfield. There are also many local merchants—Filia's Greek and American food, Pease's Candy, and The Mustard Seed Christian gift shop, for example—that give a hometown feel to this uptown retail center. The innovative White Oaks' Retail Development Program offers small or start-up ventures the full advantage of a mall location with high traffic and exposure without a long-term commitment. Everything from a cart location in the mall's common area aimed at beginning ventures, all the way through full in-line retail space for more established firms, is available.

White Oaks has become a new "town square" and setting of countless seasonal, charitable, and social activities. Early morning finds crowds of visitors who come to walk in a comfortable indoor environment. A warm family atmosphere permeates community events that include the Christmas, Easter, and Halloween seasons, musical entertainment, craft and antique fairs, safety expos, and other special events. Kids of all ages enjoy the authentic 1933 antique double-deck carousel in the center court cart market that has become a White Oaks insignia.

White Oaks has continued to flourish amidst competition. White Oaks Mall was joined by White Oaks Plaza in 1986, a modern strip-mall with a slightly different shopping focus. White Oaks Mall was completely transformed through a $7.5 million renovation in 1993 with the addition of the 475-seat food court and complete interior updating. MCL Cafeteria, which opened with the mall, is among several long-term tenants including Radio Shack, Helzberg Diamonds, and Sears.

Almost a small community in itself, White Oaks Mall offers dining, entertainment, clothing, and personal services like haircuts, nails, and banking. From a cosmetic makeover to picking up a hammer and nails for home improvement, White Oaks Mall has defined shopping for generations in central Illinois.

White Oaks Mall's Center Court Cart Marketplace offers entrepreneurs an ideal location to test new products. Photo by Randy Squires

Enterprise Index

Brandt Consolidated, Inc.
211 West Route 125
Pleasant Plains, Illinois 62677
Phone: 217-626-1123
Fax: 217-626-1927
www.brandtconsolidated.com
Pages 114-115

CIBER
Springfield, Illinois
Phone: 217-787-8917
Fax: 217-787-7392
E-mail: jmarchizza@ciber.com
www.ciber.com
Page 106

CILCO
409 West Edwards
Springfield, Illinois 62704
Phone: 217-753-5513
Fax: 217-753-5787
E-mail: lnelson@cilco.com
www.cilco.com
Page 110

Cingular Wireless
5020 Ash Grove
Springfield, Illinois 62707
Phone: 217-843-7331
Fax: 217-843-3018
E-mail: kristen.mccaw@cingular.com
Pages 104-105

Doctors Hospital
5230 South 6th Street
Springfield, Illinois 62794
Phone: 217-529-7151
Fax: 217-529-9472
www.dochos.com
Page 146

Express Personnel Services
3000 Professional Drive
Springfield, Illinois 62703
Phone: 217-528-3000
Fax: 217-528-3400
www.expresspersonnel.com
Pages 124-125

FWAI Architects Inc.
One Northwest Old Capitol Plaza
Springfield, Illinois 62701
Phone: 217-528-3661
Fax: 217-528-4717
E-mail: fwai@eosinc.com
www.fwai.com
Pages 156-157

The Greater Springfield Chamber of Commerce
3 South Old Capitol Plaza
Springfield, Illinois 62701
Phone: 217-525-1173
Fax: 217-525-8768
www.gscc.org
Pages 126-127

Hanson Professional Services Inc.
1525 South 6th Street
Springfield, Illinois 62707
Phone: 217-788-2450
Fax: 217-788-2503
E-mail: jfreitag@hanson-inc.com
www.hanson-inc.com
Pages 132-133

HIP Advertising
1125 South Fifth Street
Springfield, Illinois 62703
Phone: 217-789-4447
Fax: 217-789-4441
www.hipadvertising.com
Page 136

The Horace Mann Companies
1 Horace Mann Plaza
Springfield, Illinois 62715
Phone: 217-789-2500
Fax: 217-788-5161
www.horacemann.com
Page 140

Illinois National Bank
322 East Capitol Avenue
Springfield, Illinois 62701
Phone: 217-747-5500
Fax: 217-747-5500
www.illinoisnationalbank.com
Page 137

Insight Communications
711 South Dirksen Parkway
Springfield, Illinois 62703
Phone: 217-788-5656
Fax: 217-788-8093
www.insight-com.com
Pages 102-103

Kerber, Eck & Braeckel LLP
1000 Myers Building
1 West Old State Capitol Plaza
Springfield, Illinois 62701
Phone: 217-789-0960
Fax: 217-789-2822
E-mail: darinj@spfld.kebcpa.com
www.kebcpa.com
Pages 128-129

Kirlin-Egan & Butler Funeral Home and Cremation Tribute Center
900 South 6th Street
Springfield, Illinois 62703
Phone: 217-544-4646
         877-724-6381
Fax: 217-528-8537
E-mail: info@kirlin-egan-butler.com
www.kirlin-egan-butler.com
Page 138

Levi, Ray & Shoup, Inc.
2401 West Monroe Street
Springfield, Illinois 62704
Phone: 217-793-3800
Fax: 217-787-3286
www.lrs.com
Page 108

Lincoln Land Community College
5250 Shepherd Road
PO Box 19256
Springfield, IL 62794-9256
Phone: 217-786-2200
         800-727-4161
Fax: 217-786-2829 (public information office)
E-mail: pio@llcc.cc.il.us
www.lincolnland.net
Page 147

Mel-O-Cream Donuts International
5456 International Parkway
Springfield, Illinois 62707
Phone: 217-483-7272
Fax: 217-483-7744
www.mel-o-cream.com
Page 119

Nudo Products, Inc.
1500 Taylor Avenue
Springfield, Illinois 62703
Phone: 217-528-5636
Fax: 217-528-8722
E-mail: info@nudo.com
www.nudo.com
Pages 116-117

Orchard Park Apartments
1516 Seven Pines Road, Suite A
Springfield, Illinois 62704
Phone: 217-787-2288
Fax: 217-787-8210
Pages 158-159

P.H. Broughton & Sons, Inc.
905 North Lincoln Avenue
Springfield, Illinois 62702
Phone: 217-793-0262
Fax: 217-793-4049
Page 163

Perry Broughton Trucking & Excavating, Inc.
1227 West Enos
Springfield, Illinois 62702
Phone: 217-793-0262
Fax: 217-793-4049
Page 161

Phoenix International
5300 Rising Moon Road
Springfield, Illinois 62707
Phone: 217-483-9050
Fax: 217-483-9049
E-mail: hrspringfield@phoeintl.com
www.phoeintl.com
Page 120

R.D. Lawrence Construction Company, LTD.
603 North Amos
Springfield, Illinois 62702
Phone: 217-787-1384
Fax: 217-787-3856
E-mail: info@rdlawrence.com
www.rdlawrence.com
Page 160

Renaissance Hotel
701 East Adams Street
Springfield, Illinois 62701
Phone: 217-544-8800
Fax: 217-544-8079
www.renaissancehotels.com
Pages 166-167

Resource One
321 East Adams
Springfield, Illinois 62701
Phone: 217-753-5742
Fax: 217-753-5748
E-mail: cdavis@resource1-4u.com
www.resource1-4u.com
Page 135

Robert Morris College
3101 Montvale Drive
Springfield, Illinois 62704
Phone: 217-793-2500
www.robertmorris.edu
Page 148

Siciliano, Inc.
3650 Winchester Road
Springfield, Illinois 62707
Phone: 217-585-1200
Fax: 217-585-1211
E-mail: buildit@sicilianoinc.com
www.sicilianoinc.com
Pages 152-155

Solomon Colors
4050 Color Plant Road
Springfield, Illinois 62702
Phone: 217-522-3112
Fax: 217-522-3145
E-mail: rsolomon@solomoncolors.com
www.solomoncolors.com
Page 118

Sorling, Northrup, Hanna, Cullen and Cochran, Ltd.
Suite 800 Illinois Building
607 East Adams Street
PO Box 5131
Springfield, Illinois 62705
Phone: 217-544-1144
Fax: 217-522-3173
E-mail: businessdevelopment@sorlinglaw.com
www.sorlinglaw.com
Pages 130-131

Springfield Convention and Visitors Bureau
109 North Seventh Street
Springfield, Illinois 62701
Phone: 217-789-2360
        800-545-7300
Fax: 217-544-8711
E-mail: mailbox@springfield.il.us
www.visit-springfieldillinois.com
Page 168

Springfield Mass Transit District
928 South Ninth Street
Springfield, Illinois 62703
Phone: 217-522-6087
Fax: 217-789-9819
Page 107

Staab Funeral Home
1109 South Fifth Street
Springfield, Illinois 62703
Phone: 217-528-6461
        800-728-6461
Fax: 217-528-9016
E-mail: staab@fgi.net
www.staabfuneralhome.com
Page 134

Standard Mutual Insurance Company
1028 South Grand Avenue West
Springfield, Illinois 62704
Phone: 217-546-2894
www.standardmutual.com
Page 139

Systemax Corporation
4501 Alex Boulevard
Springfield, Illinois 62707
Phone: 217-546-6646
Fax: 217-546-6656
www.atmsupplies.com
Page 141

University of Illinois at Springfield
4900 Shepherd Road
Springfield, Illinois 62794-9243
Phone: 217-206-6600
www.uis.edu
Pages 144-145

Vancil Contracting Inc.
3900 Peoria Road
Springfield, Illinois 62702
Phone: 217-744-0442
Fax: 217-744-0443
E-mail: rv@vancon-inc.com
www.vancon-inc.com
Page 162

White Oaks Mall
2501 Wabash Avenue
Springfield, Illinois 62704
Phone: 217-787-0110
Fax: 217-787-8579
E-mail: whiteoaksmall@simon.com
www.shopsimon.com
Page 169

Yevich, Lawson and Associates, Inc.
340 West Miller Street
Springfield, Illinois 62702
Phone: 217-744-0000
        888-746-5049
Fax: 217-744-8963
E-mail: info@ylassoc.com
www.ylassoc.com
Page 109

Bibliography

Angle, Paul M. *"Here I have Lived." A History of Lincoln's Springfield, 1831-1865*. Springfield, Illinois: Abraham Lincoln Association, 1935.

Cooke, Sister M. Francis, O.S.F. *Doors That Never Close*. Springfield, Illinois Sangamon County Historical Society, 1975.

Davis, Cullom. *Memorial Days A History of Community Partnerships, 1897-1997*. Springfield, Illinois: Memorial Health Systems, 1997.

Economic Development Council for Springfield and Sangamon County. *Trends: A Demographic and Socio-economic Summary of Springfield and Sangamon County*. Springfield, Illinois: Economic Development Council, 2001.

Krohe, James, Jr. ed. *A Springfield Reader: Historical Views of the Illinois Capital, 1818-1976*. Springfield, Illinois: Sangamon County Historical Society, 1976.

Murphy, Michael P. *Greater Springfield, Building on the Legacy*. Chatsworth, California: Windsor Publications, 1993.

Office of Economic Development. *Springfield Strategy 2020: a Guide to the Future of Springfield, Past, Present, Future*. Springfield, Illinois: Office of Economic Development, 2000.

Russo, Edward J. *Prairie of Promise, Springfield and Sangamon County*. Woodland Hills, California: Windsor Publications, 1983.

Sangamon Valley Collection. Vertical Files. Springfield, Illinois: Lincoln Library.

Index

A

Abraham Lincoln Presidential Library, 21, 145, 152, 155, 167
Abraham Lincoln University, 57
Adams Wildlife Sanctuary, 77
agriculture, 37, 44, 56, 114-115
Allen Crowe Memorial 100 Race, 77
Altrusa, 90
American Association of University Women, 90
American Red Cross, 88
architecture, 37, 76, 139, 147, 157, 166
Aristocracy Hill, 27, 34-35

B

Boys and Girls Club of Springfield, 90
Brandt Consolidated, Inc., 4, 29, 114-115, 170
Bressmer Department Store, 28
Bunn, Jacob, 45

C

calhoun, 26
Calvary Academy, 57
Capital Airport, 50, 127, 163, 167
Capital Area Career Center, 56
Capitol Avenue, 35, 137
Capitol Community Health Center, 69
Capitol Complex, 34-36, 38, 58, 154
Carillon Festival, 80
Cathedral Church of Saint Paul, 89
Cathedral of the Immaculate Conception, 94
Catholic Charities, 88
Centennial Park, 77
Chatham, 60
Chest Pain Center, 69
Children of the Light Messianic Congregation, 89
Christ Episcopal, 89
CIBER, 106, 170
CILCO, 110, 170
Cingular Wireless, 104-105, 170
City Hall, 30
Claypool's drug store, 26
Concordia Theological Seminary, 57
corn, 47
Cox, Thomas, 26

D

Dana-Thomas House, 30, 48, 152-153, 157, 162
David Prince Sanitarium, 66
dentistry, 67
Discovery Room, 78
Doctors Hospital, 69, 146, 170
Dodd's Drug Store, 26

E

Eastern Star, 90
economy, 8, 11, 13, 26, 37, 43-46, 48, 66, 69, 76, 116, 127, 131-132, 144, 168, 170, 173
Elks, 90

Enos Park Neighborhood, 89
Enos, Pascal P., 26
Episcopal Diocese, 89
Ethnic Festival, 80
Ethnic Village, 80
Express Personnel Services, 4, 49, 124-125, 170

F

Family Service Center, 89
farmland, 44
federal land office, 26
Ferris Wheel, 76
festivals, 75-76, 78, 80
Fifth Street Renaissance, 89
firefighters, 89
First National Bank, 45
First Night Springfield, 78
First Presbyterian Church, 18
Freeman-Hughes House, 27
Friend in Deed, 89
Frontiers International, 90
FWAI Architects Inc., 156-157, 170

G

Gables shopping complex, 91
Goodwill, 88, 103
Great Depression, 30, 45, 119

H

Habitat for Humanity, 9, 88, 91
Hall, Carroll C., 46
Hanson Professional Services Inc., 132-133, 170
Harvard Park, 30, 89
Hawthorne Place, 89
Helping Hands, 88
Herndon, William H., 21
HIP Advertising, 136, 170
Hope School, 57, 155
hospice, 69
hospital, 59-60, 66-67, 69, 89-90, 143, 146, 160-161
House Divided Speech, 18-19

I

Iles, Elijah, 26, 48
Illinois Department of Transportation, 38, 107, 161
Illinois Executive Mansion, 35, 41
Illinois General Assembly, 34, 130
Illinois National Bank, 45-46, 137, 170
Illinois National Guard, 37
Illinois State Archives, 35
Illinois State Bank, 45
Illinois State Fair, 8, 19, 44, 76, 78-80, 107, 110, 168
Illinois State Fairgrounds, 30, 37, 78, 152, 155
Illinois State Library, 35, 58
Illinois State Museum, 35, 78
Illinois State Police, 34
Illinois State University, 57
Illinois Supreme Court Building, 35

Illinois Symphony Orchestra, 78, 110
Illinois Vietnam Veterans Memorial, 77
Insight Communications, 102-103, 170
International Route 66 Mother Road Festival, 80
interpreters, 21, 29, 34
Iron Horse Triathlon, 84

J

Jaycees, 90
Junior Blues, 77, 84, 110

K

Kerber, Eck & Braeckel LLP, 128-129, 170
Kirlin-Egan & Butler Funeral Home and Cremation Tribute Center, 138, 170
Kiwanis, 90
Knights of Columbus, 90
Korean War Memorial, 76-77

L

Lake Shore Improvement, 89
Lake Springfield, 30, 62, 77, 84, 126-127, 160, 162-163
Lamb, James L., 44
Land of Lincoln Legal Assistance Foundation, 90
League of Women Voters, 90
Legislative Reference Bureau, 58
Levi, Ray & Shoup, Inc., 108, 170
Liebling, A.J., 21
Lincoln, Abraham, 8, 11, 18-22, 25, 28, 30, 34, 57, 80, 126, 144-145, 152-155, 167-168, 172
Lincoln-Herndon law offices, 21
Lincoln Home National Historic District, 29
Lincoln Land Community College, 58, 77, 110, 132, 147, 162, 170
Lincoln Library, 13, 22, 26, 28, 162, 172
Lincoln, Mary, 19, 167
Lincoln Memorial Garden, 77
Lincoln Presidential Library and Museum, 78, 145, 155
Lincoln, Robert Todd, 19-20
Lindsay Place, 89
Lions, 90
Little League, 88
Lost Bridge Trail, 77
LPGA State Farm Classic, 78, 105, 108

M

manufacturing, 9, 27, 30, 43-46, 106, 113, 116, 120, 126-127
Masonic Temple, 78
Masons, 90
Matheny, Charles, 37
Mather and Wells, 89
Matteson, Joel, 34
McFarland Mental Health Center, 37, 157
Meals on Wheels, 90
Mel-O-Cream Donuts International, 119, 170
Memorial Medical Center, 59, 66-67
Michael J. Howlett Building, 35
midway, 8, 79
Mini O'Beirne Crisis Nursery, 89, 106

Monroe Street, 26-28, 48, 108
Muni Opera, 78
Municipal Opera, 62

N

National Association for the Advancement of Colored People (NAACP), 30
National Prohibition Act, 30
neighborhood associations, 89
neighborhoods, 27, 30, 46, 87
Nelson Center, 76, 84, 162
New Salem, 21, 25, 29, 80, 91, 152-154
Nimmo, Leslie W., 46
Nineteenth Century Children's Fair, 21
North End, 27, 89
Northern Cross Railroad, 26
Nudo Products, Inc., 116-117, 170

O

O'Connor, Andrew, 17
Odd fellows, 90
old Chicago and Alton depot, 28
Old State Capitol, 18-19, 34, 127, 152, 154
Optimists, 90
Orchard Park Apartments, 158-159, 170
Orpheum Theater, 27

P

P.H. Broughton & Sons, Inc., 163, 171
parade, 18, 92, 170, 173
parks, 75-77, 79, 168, 170, 173
Perry Broughton Trucking & Excavating, Inc., 161, 171
Petah Tikvah Messianic Jewish Congregation, 89
Phoenix International, 120, 171
Pleasant Plains, 60, 114, 162
police, 27, 30, 34, 89
politics, 30, 34, 36, 41
PORA, 90
private schools, 30, 55

R

R.D. Lawrence Construction Company, LTD., 160, 171
Rabbit Row, 27
Rague, John, 34
railroads, 26-27, 44
recreation, 51, 57, 75-76, 79
Rees Memorial Carillon, 76
rehabilitation, 68, 146
Renaissance Hotel, 166-167, 171
Resource One, 135, 171
Ridgley Bank, 26, 28
Robert Morris College, 60, 148, 171
Rochester, 60, 77, 162
Roman Catholic diocese, 94
Ronald McDonald House, 88, 105
Rotary, 90
Route 66 museum, 78

S

Sacred Heart-Griffin, 57
Saint Luke's Episcopal, 89
Salvation Army, 88
Sangamon Auditorium, 8, 63, 78, 110, 144-145
Sangamon Auditorium Concert Series, 78
Sangamon County, 26, 34, 37-38, 69-70, 80, 90, 126-127, 157, 172
Sangamon County Complex, 38, 157
Sangamon County Courthouse, 34
Sangamon County Fair, 80
Sangamon Insurance Company, 46
Sangamon River, 21, 26
Sangamon State University, 58, 61, 127, 158
Sangamon Valley Collection, 13, 172
Saturday Evening Post, 30
Saunders, William, 77
Sertoma, 90
Sherman, 60, 78
Shriners, 90
Siciliano, Inc., 4, 92, 152-155, 171
Simonds, O.C., 76
Solomon Colors, 118, 171
Sorling, Northrup, Hanna, Cullen and Cochran, Ltd., 130-131, 171
Southeast High School, 56
Southern Illinois Trauma Center, 67
Southern Illinois University's School of Medicine, 59
Southtown, 27
soybean, 47
Springfield Area Arts Council, 78
Springfield Art Association, 30, 78
Springfield Ballet Company, 62
Springfield Children's Museum, 78
Springfield Clinic, 69
Springfield College, 58, 77
Springfield Community Foundation, 89
Springfield Convention and Visitors Bureau, 168, 171
Springfield Hospital and Training School, 66-67
Springfield Mass Transit District, 48, 107, 171
Springfield Mile, 77
Springfield Park District, 76
Springfield public school system, 56
Springfield Theatre Guild, 78
St. John's Breadline, 88
St. John's Hospital, 59-60, 66
St. Mary's Church, 57
Staab Funeral Home, 134, 171
Standard Mutual Insurance Company, 139, 171
State Historical Library, 21, 58
State of Illinois, 8, 19-21, 26, 34, 37-38, 48, 135, 137, 152-154
suburbs, 46, 60
Sunday, Billy, 30
Systemax Corporation, 141, 171

T

Talisman, 26
Temple B'rith Sholom, 89
Temple Israel, 89
The Greater Springfield Chamber of Commerce, 2, 4, 11, 13, 110, 126-127, 170
The Horace Mann Companies, 46, 140, 170
The Mather Grove, 34
The North End Improvement, 89
The State Journal-Register, 21, 50, 110
Theatre Centre, 62

U

United Way, 88, 105
University of Illinois at Springfield, 56, 58-59, 61, 63, 78, 110, 144-145, 171
Ursuline Academy, 57

V

Vancil Contracting Inc., 162, 171
Vandalia, 34
veterans, 37, 69, 77-78, 90, 127, 134
Veterans Administration Clinic, 69
Vinegar Hill, 27
volunteer, 88-90, 105, 110, 131, 139

W

Wabash Railroad Hospital, 66
Washington Park, 8, 76
Washington Street Jazz Festival, 80
Washington Street Mission, 91
West Side neighborhood, 89
Westchester, 89
White Oaks Mall, 46, 169, 171
Williams, John, 45
World War I, 28
World War II, 30, 119, 163
WQNA-FM, 56
Wright, Frank Lloyd, 153

Y

Yevich, Lawson and Associates, Inc., 109, 171